A Dialogue on Free Will and Science

Alfred R. Mele
Florida State University

New York   Oxford
OXFORD UNIVERSITY PRESS

Oxford University Press is a department of the University of Oxford.
It furthers the University's objective of excellence in research,
scholarship, and education by publishing worldwide.

Oxford New York
Auckland Cape Town Dar es Salaam Hong Kong Karachi
Kuala Lumpur Madrid Melbourne Mexico City Nairobi
New Delhi Shanghai Taipei Toronto

With offices in
Argentina Austria Brazil Chile Czech Republic France Greece
Guatemala Hungary Italy Japan Poland Portugal Singapore
South Korea Switzerland Thailand Turkey Ukraine Vietnam

Copyright © 2014 by Oxford University Press

Published by Oxford University Press
198 Madison Avenue, New York, New York 10016
http://www.oup.com

Oxford is a registered trademark of Oxford University Press

Library of Congress Cataloging-in-Publication Data
Mele, Alfred R., 1951-
    A dialogue on free will and science / Alfred R. Mele.
      pages cm
    Includes index.
    ISBN 978-0-19-932929-8
1. Free will and determinism—Miscellanea. 2. Imaginary conversations.
    I. Title. BJ1461.M45   2013
    123'.5—dc23   2013016322

Printing number: 9 8 7 6 5 4 3 2 1
Printed in the United States of America
on acid-free paper

For my children again (but this time in chronological order):
Al, Nick, and Angela.

Contents

Preface

One day, my son Nick and I were talking about how I might write a book for undergraduates or even a more general audience on scientific challenges to free will. After some discussion—and at the same moment, it seemed—we had the same thought: I should write a dialogue. And I did. I enjoyed the process very much. The result is this book, which I hope you will enjoy.

I see philosophy as an adventure. You start with a philosophical question and try to work out a defensible answer. Your initial question leads to other questions that need answers too. Sometimes you can't see what's coming next—what question, what problem, what answer. And that can make the process exciting. An ordinary way of writing a philosophy book for students can dampen the excitement a bit: In each chapter, you begin by telling your readers what you are going to do and how you are going to do it; then you do it; and then you remind them what you did. In a dialogue, ideas can emerge and be clarified and evaluated in a more natural way that can make the process more engaging, more enjoyable, and more exciting.

After they try to come to grips with what having free will might involve, my characters describe and react to the experiments that are often said to pose the greatest scientific challenges to the existence of free will. Some of the experiments come from neuroscience and others from social psychology. The guiding question of the dialogue is this: How much power do the leading scientific challenges to free will have? For example, are they so powerful that all educated people should be skeptical about free will? Do they perhaps point to limitations on free will without justifying skepticism about the existence of free will? A lot of what my characters have to say responds directly to my guiding question. My primary goal is to help readers evaluate the scientific challenges to free will and to answer my guiding question for themselves.

For comments on a draft of this book, I am grateful to Joe Campbell, Washington State University; Rami El Ali, University of Miami; Andreas Falke, University of Florida; Meghan Griffith, Davidson College; Stephen Kearns, Florida State University; Benjamin McMyler, Texas A&M University; Chris Meyers, University of Southern Mississippi; Jason Miller, Florida State University; Eddy Nahmias, Georgia State University; Josh Shepherd, Florida State University; Bruce Waller, Youngstown State University. I owe a special debt to Andrei Buckareff, of Marist College, who gave a draft of the book a trial run in a course. Andrei forwarded his students' comments to me and sent advice of his own. I am grateful to Josh Shepherd for the initial drafts of the diagrams and to Angela Mele for the cover art and comments on an early draft. This book was made possible through the support of a grant from the John Templeton Foundation. The opinions expressed here do not necessarily reflect the views of the John Templeton Foundation.

1

Monday Afternoon

Scene: Alice is reading a news article on her laptop in her favorite coffee shop.

BOB: Here you go, Alice. A caramel kiss frappé. Just the thing for a Tallahassee summer afternoon.

ALICE: Perfect, thanks. The next one's on me.

BOB: What are you reading?

ALICE: An article about how a team of neuroscientists proved that free will is an illusion.

BOB: Do you believe it?

ALICE: No, but . . .

BOB: Do you believe in free will?

ALICE: Well, suppose I said yes. I'm not sure how much that would tell you about me. Maybe what I mean by "free will" isn't what you mean by it. In fact, maybe what I mean by it isn't what the neuroscientists meant by it. And maybe the scientists and the journalist mean different things by it too.

BOB: What does the team of neuroscientists mean by "free will"?

ALICE: I don't know. The article doesn't say. It doesn't say what the journalist means either—or what anyone means by it.

BOB: OK. So why don't you tell me what *you* mean by "free will"?

ALICE: I'm not sure, exactly. Last semester, I took Intro to Philosophy. We didn't study free will, but we studied lots of interesting topics— knowledge, for example. The professor—I forget her name—asked us to define "knowledge" for her. She put it this way: What does it mean to say that "S knows that p." Anyway . . .

BOB: So what does "S knows that p" mean?

ALICE: Come to think of it, maybe she wasn't a professor after all. She was pretty young—maybe a grad student.

BOB: Back to "S knows that p." Can we make it "Sam knows that a professor taught your philosophy course"?

ALICE: Sure. Now, you might think it's enough for Sam to know this that he believes it and it's true. So you might say that for S to know that p is for S to believe that p when p is true. But imagine that Sam believes that a professor taught the course only because he doesn't realize that some of our courses are taught by grad students and not professors. He thinks that all of our courses are taught by professors; so he infers that what's-her-name was a professor. Then, we might say, for all Sam *knew*, his teacher might have been a grad student rather than a professor.

BOB: I see. Sam didn't know that the course was taught by a professor— even if it was—because he can't tell the difference between professors who teach courses and grad students who teach courses.

ALICE: Something like that. Sam didn't have a good reason to believe that the teacher was a professor rather than a grad student. Or, as the teacher used to like to put it, he wasn't *justified* in believing that she was a professor. She used the word "justified" a lot.

BOB: Well, then, can we say that knowledge is justified true belief?

ALICE: I suppose. But then we have to ask how much justification you need. I seem to recall that a crazy brain-in-a-vat story came in here.

BOB: What story?

ALICE: Oh, fifty years ago, the surface of the earth was destroyed in a nuclear war. But just before that happened, a neuroscientist took your brain out of your head, put it in a vat of life-sustaining liquid, and hooked your brain up to a computer program that flooded it with a long series of experiences that are indistinguishable from real-life experiences. Then her staff put the vat and the computer in a deep hole and covered it up.

BOB: Hey, that reminds me of *The Matrix*, a truly excellent movie. Is that where your professor—teacher, excuse me—got the idea?

ALICE: No, it came from a philosophy professor named Hilary Putnam long before *The Matrix* was conceived.

BOB: Anyway, the story is crazy. I'm only twenty years old. So my brain can't have been taken out of my body fifty years ago. Case closed.

ALICE: How do you know?

BOB: How do I know what? That I'm twenty?

ALICE: Yes.

BOB: I carry a little copy of my birth certificate in my wallet. Here, take a look.

Alice pretends to scrutinize the birth certificate.

ALICE: How do you know that's your birth certificate?

BOB: Are you suggesting it's a forgery?

ALICE: No. I'm . . .

BOB: Oh, I see. How do I know it's a birth certificate at all? If the crazy story is true, then my experience of a birth certificate is just a product of the program. There's no birth certificate at all in my hand. In fact, I don't have a hand. We're not in a coffee shop, and . . .

ALICE: Right. And how do you know the crazy story *isn't* true? If you don't know that, then you don't know you're too young for it to be true.

Alice and Bob see a friend approaching.

CLIFF: Hey! What's going on?

BOB: Hi Cliff. We started talking about whether a team of neuroscientists had proved there's no free will, but somehow we got on to *The Matrix*.

CLIFF: Ah, *The Matrix*. Will you choose the red pill or the blue pill? Remember that bit, when Neo needs to make the big decision. That's serious free will stuff.

ALICE: Maybe so. But what I was leading up to in talking about a thought experiment that reminded Bob of *The Matrix* was just a general point about words. We tend to think we know what we mean by some words—words like "know," "good," and "fair," for example—until we start to think a bit about what we mean. I was making that point about "know" with a *Matrix*-like thought experiment, and I was going to suggest that "free will" might be like this. Maybe we won't have a good idea what we mean by "free will" until we try to give a definition of it. Or if not a definition, at least something pretty close.

CLIFF: I see. At least I think I do. I'll tell you what I mean by "free will": being able to do what you want.

BOB: Do you mean being able to do *whatever* you want? When I was a kid I wanted to fly like Superman and leap tall buildings in a single bound. Of course, I've never been able to do these things. Does that mean I didn't have free will when I was a kid?

CLIFF: Well, I guess that would be super free will. I'll change what I said. How about this? You have free will about something you want to do if you're able to do it. So you didn't have free will about flying like Superman, but I have free will about ordering a caramel kiss frappé. I want to order one, and I'm able to do that. Just wait and see.

ALICE: But you've always said you hate frappés. What's going on? Why do you want one now?

CLIFF: You're right. And I was about to order one. What *is* going on?

BOB: Would you like me to get a frappé for you, Cliff?

CLIFF: Now, wait. This is weird. I just came from a hypnosis experiment. The hypnotist told me I might find myself wanting to do something— something harmless, she said—that I'd never wanted to do before. I'll bet this is it.

ALICE: So do you think you have free will about ordering a frappé?

CLIFF: Maybe I do now that it occurred to me why I have this unusual urge for a frappé. But if I had just gone ahead and ordered one earlier, I think her hypnosis would have been at work rather than my free will.

BOB: So would you like to change your definition of free will again? I think there are some other reasons to change it too. Imagine that when you're walking around tonight, a terrifying man threatens to shoot you unless you hand over your money and cell phone. You want to hand them over in order to get him not to shoot you, and you're able to do that. But do you have free will about giving him your money and phone?

CLIFF: I'm not sure. But I see this is complicated. I thought I knew what "free will" meant, but now I'm feeling confused. I guess this is what Alice was talking about. Let me take a break from this philosophizing and figure out what to drink.

ALICE: Do you still want the frappé?

CLIFF: I do. But I'm going to order my normal latte. Even if the hypnotist made me want the frappé, I doubt she can make me *enjoy* it.

As Cliff walks away to order his latte, another friend, Deb, pulls up a chair.

DEB: Cliff looks strange: bewildered, I'd say. What's up with him?

BOB: He was in a hypnosis experiment today. That's probably it. But we were also talking about free will, and that has me a bit bewildered. Maybe our discussion had the same effect on Cliff.

DEB: Free will, eh. Do we have it?

ALICE: We didn't get nearly that far, though that's close to where we started. We were talking about what "free will" might mean.

DEB: What a coincidence! This morning I read a short article by a philosophy professor in the *Phi Kappa Phi Forum* on just this topic. It's still in my backpack.

Cliff returns while Deb digs out the magazine. He's sipping a frappé.

CLIFF: I knew I wouldn't like this frappé.

BOB: Why did you order it? I thought you decided on a latte.

CLIFF: Oh, I decided in the end to flip a coin, and it came up frappé. Are you still talking about free will?

ALICE: Yep. And Deb is about to tell us what a philosophy professor says about it.

CLIFF: What's her name?

DEB: His. Alfred Mele.

CLIFF: Never heard of him.

ALICE: Well, I've never heard of him either, but what does he say?

DEB: He describes three different ways of understanding what "free will" means, using a gas station analogy. There's regular, mid-grade, and premium gas, and there are regular, mid-grade, and premium meanings for free will.

CLIFF: So some meanings are more expensive than others, or what?

BOB: Hey, shouldn't free will be free, or at least cheap? Gas is expensive.

ALICE: Let's hear what the philosopher has to say.

DEB: It's a short article, and the author isn't filling in the details, but maybe we can do that ourselves.

ALICE: We'll see.

DEB: The least expensive meaning of "free will" has to do with being a competent decision maker who hasn't been manipulated and isn't being compelled or coerced. The person isn't hypnotized, no one is holding a gun to his head, or threatening him, and so on. He needs to make up his mind about something—say, how to spend his evening—is capable of making an informed decision about that, and makes one. He weighs up reasons—pros and cons—and decides on that basis.

CLIFF: Hey, what should *we* do tonight?

ALICE: We can decide later, Cliff.

CLIFF: OK. Back to philosophy. This free will sounds really cheap. If that's all there is to it, we all have it. Right? What about the old free will versus determinism thing? If determinism is true, there can still be competent decision makers who make informed decisions, and normally people aren't hypnotized or being threatened. But wouldn't determinism rule out free will anyway?

BOB: What do you mean by "determinism," Cliff?

CLIFF: Here's how my high school physics teacher explained it to me a couple of years ago. It's the idea that a complete description of the universe at any time—fifty years ago, shortly after the Big Bang, or whatever—together with a complete list of all the laws of nature entails everything else that's true about the universe, including everything that will ever happen.

BOB: What do you mean by "entails"?

CLIFF: The basic idea is this: One statement entails another when, necessarily, if the first statement is true, then so is the second. We ask, "Does statement A entail statement B?" If there's no possible way for the first statement to be true without the second one being true, then the answer is yes. So let statement A be a complete description of the universe a billion years ago together with a complete list of all the laws of nature, and let statement B be that Ed will walk in and say "Hey" ten seconds from now . . .

Another friend, Ed, walks into the coffee shop.

ED: Hey.

Bob: You saw him coming, Cliff. You don't fool me.

Cliff: Maybe and maybe not, Bob. Hey, Ed. Pull up a chair.

Deb: Hi, Ed. Cliff, finish your sentence please. I think I have it, but I want to be sure.

Cliff: I'll finish my sentence in a different tense. If determinism is true, then there's no possible way for statement A in my sentence to be true without it also being true that Ed would walk in here when he did.

Bob: Does determinism force you to do things then?

Cliff: Not at all. Determinism isn't a force. It's just a way a universe is if a statement about it like statement A entails all the other true statements about it. Here's another example of entailment—one that doesn't have anything to do with determinism or free will. Let statement A be "There are tables and chairs here," and let statement B be "There are tables here." Statement A entails statement B because there's no way A can be true without B being true.

Ed: What are you guys talking about?

Alice: It all started when I told Bob I was reading an article about how a team of neuroscientists proved that we don't have free will. Eventually, we began talking about what "free will" might mean, and Deb started telling us about an article she read about this. The author is a philosophy professor. He talks about three different meanings for "free will." Deb described one of them, and Cliff said it falls short of free will because it doesn't rule out determinism.

Ed: Ah, yes, *compatibilism*—the view that free will is compatible with determinism.

Bob: Did you make that term up just now?

Ed: No, I learned it in a philosophy course. Philosophy professors like p's, q's, and isms.

Bob: Can you tell the difference between philosophy professors and grad students who teach philosophy courses?

Ed: What?

Alice: OK, boys. Can we move on to this philosophy professor's second meaning for "free will," the analog of mid-grade gas at his philosophical gas station? Deb, what did he say?

Deb: He realized that some—perhaps many—people would not accept what Ed called compatibilism. So he tried to describe a meaning for "free will" that makes it incompatible with determinism. Here he mixed what he called "deep openness" into "regular" free will.

ALICE: What did he have in mind?

DEB: It starts like this. Sometimes, if things had been a bit different, you would have made a different decision than you actually did. For example, if Cliff had been in a slightly better mood, he might have decided to buy Ed a coffee. But this isn't enough for *deep* openness. What you need is that more than one option was open to you, given everything as it actually was at the time—your mood, all your thoughts and feelings, your brain, your environment, and, indeed, the entire universe and its entire history.

CLIFF: So part of what he's saying is that you don't have this kind of free will if determinism is true. If determinism is true, you might have made a different decision if things had been a bit different before you decided; say, if you had been in a better—or worse—mood. Of course, if determinism is true, things couldn't have been a bit different, given what already happened. But . . .

ED: That's just shallow openness, I guess.

CLIFF: Right. And as I was going to say, if determinism is true, you can't make a different decision if things are exactly the same before you decide. But if determinism is false, the door is open to deep openness.

DEB: That's the idea. This second meaning of "free will" adds to the first one. So again we think about a competent decision maker who isn't being manipulated, compelled, or coerced, and then we add deep openness to that. If the person makes an informed decision, and if he could have made a different decision right then, he has this kind of free will at the time.

ALICE: And when you say "could have made a different decision," you don't mean that he might have made a different one if things had been a bit different before he decided, right? You're saying that he could have made a different decision in exactly the circumstances he was in.

DEB: Right.

ED: I just remembered another thing that some philosophy professors really like—possible worlds. They're sort of like parallel universes, but not exactly. Anyway, you can put the point about the decider we're talking about—call him Zeke—like this. In the actual world, Zeke decided to go to the Warehouse tonight to shoot pool; but in another possible world where everything was the same—from the Big Bang on—right up to the moment he decided to go to the Warehouse, something else happened. Maybe he decided to stay home and study instead, or kept on thinking about what to do for a while, or whatever. The important thing is that things did not have to be different at all before he decided in order for something different to happen. That's the deep openness thing.

BOB: This is sounding kind of random to me—like Zeke's brain is flipping a coin, or tossing dice, or something.

DEB: Yes, it does sound strange, but would you like me to describe the third meaning of "free will" before we talk about that?

CLIFF: Hey, maybe we should go to the Warehouse tonight. I don't know who Zeke is, but we might run into him there.

ALICE: Let's decide about tonight later. I'd like to hear about this third meaning of "free will."

BOB: OK, Deb. Go for it.

DEB: To get the third meaning, the analog of premium gas, the professor adds something to the second—a soul or mind that isn't physical.

BOB: That makes free will supernatural.

DEB: Right. The professor doesn't seem too fond of this meaning of "free will," but he puts it out there anyway.

BOB: This is getting really deep now—too deep for me. And I've got to leave soon; I need to go to work. What do you think about meeting at the Warehouse tonight?

After a bit of banter, they all agree to meet at the Warehouse around 10:00.

2
Monday Night

Scene: Alice and Bob are sitting in the Warehouse, an old pool hall and bar, waiting for their friends.

ALICE: This afternoon's discussion was fun. Which of those three different meanings of "free will" struck you as best?

BOB: I'm keeping an open mind for now. If I understood things better, I might have a different attitude about it.

ALICE: I know what you mean. I feel the same.

Deb and Cliff walk in, followed by Ed.

CLIFF: Pool anyone?

ED: It looks like it's going to rain, and the roof leaks over some of the pool tables. The water gives "pool" a different meaning. Playing water pool isn't much fun.

BOB: When you say it's going to rain, what does "it" refer to?

ED: I don't know. The sky? Maybe rain, as in "rain is raining." I can see you're in the mood for some philosophizing. Did our free will discussion do that to you?

ALICE: Bob and I were just talking about that. Did you guys like any of the three meanings of "free will" Deb described this afternoon?

CLIFF: The more I thought about it, the more I liked the first one—the one Ed called compatibilism, the analog of regular gas. It's very down to earth. Making a rational, informed decision in the absence of any monkey business seems good enough to me. If deep openness didn't seem to bring with it a weird kind of randomness, I might go for the second one instead—mid-grade free will.

BOB: But compatibilism is the idea that free will is compatible with determinism, and that's a contradiction in terms. By definition, determinism leaves no room for free will.

ED: By what definition? Maybe what some people mean by "determinism" is just "something or other that rules out free will." But I don't see how that's part of the meaning of "determinism" we talked about this afternoon.

BOB: Can you remind me?

ED: It came from Cliff's high school physics teacher. He'll remember it better than I do.

CLIFF: It's the idea that a complete description of the universe at any time—say, shortly after the Big Bang—together with a complete list of all the laws of nature entails everything else that's true about the universe, including everything that will ever happen.

BOB: Right, I remember. And you gave an example of entailment that involved Ed.

CLIFF: I did. Question: When does one statement—p, say—entail another statement; call it q? Answer: When there's no possible way for p to be true without q being true. So let p be a complete description of the universe a billion years ago together with a complete list of all the laws of nature, and let q be that Fran will walk in and say "Hi guys" ten seconds from now . . .

Another friend, Fran, walks into the old pool hall. It's raining. Two Warehouse workers, George and Tucker, cover some pool tables with tarps and place some trash cans under leaks.

FRAN: Hi guys.

BOB: Don't try the same trick twice, Cliff. You saw her coming, and you know she always says "Hi guys" when she sees us.

CLIFF: Maybe, maybe not.

BOB: Anyway, I remember. If determinism is true, then given that Fran walked in here a minute ago, there was no possible way for p to be true—that statement about the past and the laws of nature—without it also being true that Fran would walk in here then and say "Hi guys," as she always does.

FRAN: What on earth are you guys talking about?

DEB: Well, maybe it's not exactly Earth—at least not the Earth in our universe. I believe determinism is false. We're talking about free will and determinism.

FRAN: Cool, but strange—for you guys. What happened? Did someone hypnotize you?

CLIFF: I'll tell you about that another time.

BOB: OK, I can admit that it might not be just plain obvious that determinism as you define it rules out free will. But, even so, don't you really need to be able to act different than you actually do—at least sometimes—in order to have free will? For example, in order for Fran to have free will about what she says when she sees us, wouldn't she have to be able to say something other than "Hi guys"—at least sometimes?

FRAN: What are you guys talking about? Do I say "Hi guys" a lot?

General laughter.

CLIFF: About being able to act differently . . . I'm not so sure. Imagine that just after Ed walked in, Tucker and George locked the doors without our knowing it. We were sitting here happily, philosophizing away like those ancient Greeks. We stayed in the Warehouse. But we couldn't have left—at least not without finding George or Tucker and getting the door unlocked. And even so, I'd say we stayed here of our own free will. That we weren't actually able to leave at the time doesn't matter.

ALICE: That's clever. But I think of free will as being more about choosing or deciding than about staying in old pool halls with leaky roofs. Maybe we stayed here of our own free will because we chose to stay here. But we could have chosen to leave. Maybe choosing of your own free will depends on being able to choose something else instead.

BOB: But if the doors were locked, we couldn't have chosen to leave.

DEB: Sure, we could have chosen to leave. It's just that if we had tried to leave, we would have discovered that we were locked in. Sometimes we choose to do things that we don't succeed in doing. Yesterday, I chose to drive to the beach rather than to my sister's house. But I ended up not driving anywhere. My car wouldn't start.

ED: That's too bad. Is it running now?

DEB: No, it's in the shop.

FRAN: This reminds me of a story a friend of mine told me—a philosophy major. He called it a Frankfurt-style story and said it was named after a philosophy professor named Harry Frankfurt.

BOB: Hey, I know that name. I saw him on *The Daily Show* a couple of years ago. But he was talking about a book of his called *On Bullshit*, not free will. Is the story about bullshit?

FRAN: No, it's about free will.

ALICE: Let's hear it.

FRAN: There's a powerful spirit who can read your mind and tell what you're about to choose. She can also make you choose things, if she wants.

BOB: Sounds like bullshit already.

ALICE: Come on, Bob. Let's hear the story.

FRAN: This spirit doesn't like to interfere unless she has to. She wants a guy named Jones to choose to steal Deb's car. She can make him choose that just by fiddling with his brain, but she'd like it better if he made that choice on his own, without her butting in. So the spirit waits to see what Jones is about to choose, and she sees he's about to choose to steal the car. So she just hangs back and waits. Jones chooses on his own to steal Deb's car. The spirit doesn't make him make this choice. But she would have made him make it if she had seen he wasn't going to make it on his own.

CLIFF: Got it. There's no way Jones can avoid choosing to steal Deb's car. Either he makes that choice on his own or the spirit makes him make it. There's no other possibility.

BOB: But why are we supposed to think Jones had free will when he made his choice?

FRAN: I think it's supposed to go like this. First, imagine that many people in Jones's universe have free will. Then imagine that Jones has it under normal conditions. Now, Jones's situation is different when that sneaky spirit is hanging around than when she isn't. But she doesn't actually interfere. Jones made his choice in the same way he makes choices when the spirit isn't reading his mind. So if he makes choices freely in normal circumstances, he makes this one freely too.

BOB: I still don't get it.

ALICE: Here's a way to look at it, Bob. Take the spirit out of the story and leave everything else the same. Jones chooses on his own to steal Deb's car—of his own free will, or *freely*, as Fran was saying. Now, put the spirit back in the story and have her do just what she did in the story Fran told us. Well, the spirit doesn't butt in—she doesn't make Jones choose what he chooses. So putting her back in the story can't change Jones's choice from free to unfree.

BOB: OK, I get it. But how is Jones going to steal Deb's car anyway? It doesn't start; he can't drive it away.

ALICE: We're concentrating on his *choosing* to steal it. But if you want him actually to steal it too, we can make it part of the story that the car has been fixed.

DEB: Let's keep the car broken for a while. I don't want it stolen.

The friends hear people complaining that the Warehouse doors are stuck and they can't get out. It takes a while, but Tucker solves the problem. It's raining harder now.

BOB: Maybe the spirit locked the doors. What's her name anyway?

ED: Let's call her Sally—after our most spiritual friend.

ALICE: Good idea.

BOB: You know, our discussion of free will started this afternoon when Alice told me about a group of neuroscientists who proved free will is an illusion. But what we've been talking about sounds a lot more like science fiction or fantasy than science. I'm still curious about those neuroscientists.

ALICE: We'll get back to that eventually, I'm sure. But don't you agree that we need to have a pretty good idea what we mean by "free will" before we can figure out whether those scientists proved we don't have any?

BOB: I suppose so. And science fiction can be entertaining anyway.

DEB: I think I understand Fran's story. But I still feel strongly that determinism rules out free will, even when determinism means what Cliff's physics teacher says it means. What kind of universe is Fran's story set in?

If determinism is true in that universe, I say that Jones doesn't have free will even in normal circumstances—even when Sally the spirit isn't lurking nearby.

BOB: We could say that Jones's universe isn't deterministic and see what happens to the story then.

CLIFF: But won't that take us away from compatibilism and on to mid-grade free will—the idea of free will that depends on deep openness?

BOB: Maybe so.

ALICE: I agree. Deb, why are you so convinced that determinism rules out free will?

DEB: Let's try another thought experiment. Here's the story. Diana is a goddess, and determinism is true in the universe she inhabits. Lots of human beings live there too. She hasn't created any of them, but she'd like to create one now. In fact, she has written a novel that chronicles the life of a guy named Ernie from his childhood until his death at the age of eighty. In the novel, Ernie does all sorts of things, of course. She'd like to create a human being who does all those things and more.

BOB: How will she do that?

DEB: Diana knows all the laws of nature and she knows everything that was going on in her universe last week. She deduces from this knowledge that if she builds a zygote in a certain way and implants it in a certain woman—Mary—at a certain time, it will grow into Ernie and do all the things she wants Ernie to do.

BOB: How will she build it?

DEB: Oh, just by mushing atoms together in a certain way. I don't know how to do it, but Diana does.

CLIFF: And how will she implant it?

DEB: She's a goddess; she'll figure it out. And it will all work out exactly as planned. Diana's complete knowledge of the laws of nature and the state of her deterministic universe last week enables her to deduce how to produce a being who lives a life that includes doing everything Ernie does in her novel, and she has the technical skills to create him.

BOB: After Diana creates Ernie, will she need to butt in occasionally to keep him on track?

DEB: No, when she creates him she already knows everything he'll do, and she knows that he'll do it without her ever having to butt in. She deduces all this from her knowledge of the laws of nature and the condition of the universe a while before she creates Ernie.

Bob: OK. I've got it. So how does this apply to the question whether determinism rules out free will?

Deb: Recall the idea of regular free will at the philosophical gas station. It highlights being a competent decision maker who hasn't been manipulated and isn't being compelled or coerced. The person isn't hypnotized, no one is holding a gun to his head, or threatening him, and so on. He needs to make up his mind about something, is capable of making an informed decision about that, and makes one. When we understand free will this way, a person like the one I just described has free will when he makes his decision.

Ed: Right. And even if determinism is true, there can be people like this.

Deb: Good. In my story, Ernie is a person like this. So, if we understand free will in the *regular* way—the compatibilist way—we should say that Ernie does lots of things freely. But does he? What do you think?

Bob: I don't see Ernie as a free agent. He seems like Diana's tool to me. She built him to do everything he does. Once he begins to exist, he's not compelled, coerced, or manipulated. He grows into a competent decision maker who makes lots of reasonable decisions. But I don't see how any of these decisions are free.

Fran: I tend to agree. Ernie doesn't seem to have free will. He seems like a puppet, in a way—a thinking and deciding one. Anyway, how his life goes—everything he does—is preordained by Diana, just as she preordained what the Ernie in her novel would do.

Deb: So at least some of us think or feel that Ernie doesn't have free will. Let's compare Ernie with another person. Here's a new story. Back when Diana was thinking about how to create Ernie, she deduced from her knowledge of the laws of nature and the condition of her universe a week ago that a certain married couple would have—in the normal way—a baby they would name Bernie. The amazing thing is that she also deduced that Bernie would do all the things Ernie does in her novel—at exactly the same times and places. Diana didn't care about the name—in fact, she thought "Bernie" might have been a nice name for her character. So she didn't bother to create Ernie; she turned her talented mind to other endeavors instead.

Bob: So Diana didn't build Bernie. He was just a product of love, or lust, or both, as the case may be. But determinism is true in his universe. And because Diana deduced that Bernie would do everything she wanted done, she didn't bother to build Ernie. Is that right?

Ed: And we should assume that, just like Ernie, Bernie is a competent decision maker who often makes reasonable decisions and so on. Right?

Deb: Yes. Right on both counts. Now, does Bernie have free will? Is the difference between how he came to exist—that is, through ordinary sexual reproduction—and the way Ernie came to exist the kind of thing that can make the difference between having and lacking free will?

Ed: Here's a thought. I don't know how good it is. Let's assume that Bernie's and Ernie's lives go exactly the same way. Neither Ernie nor Bernie had any say about how they came to exist. Neither had any say about anything that existed before they were born. And neither had any say about the laws of nature. They're on a par there, and they do all the same things and make all the same decisions. So I'd say that either both have free will or neither does. It's true that one was built and the other was a product of sexual reproduction. But I just don't see how that single difference between them can have the consequence that although one has free will the other lacks it.

Alice: There's more to the difference between Ernie and Bernie than that. Not only was Ernie built, but he was built *to do* everything he did.

Ed: I realize that. But if it was inevitable that Ernie would do everything Diana planned for him to do, it was just as inevitable that Bernie would do all the same things. In both cases, what they would do—and decide to do, of course—was dictated by the combination of the laws of nature and the condition of the universe long ago. In light of that, I'd say they're equally unfree.

Cliff: I have a different perspective on Ernie and Bernie. As I think of free will, it's something we need in order to be morally responsible for things we do. By being morally responsible, I mean something like this: deserving to be blamed from a moral point of view for some bad action you performed or deserving some credit from that point of view for a good action you performed. So if Bernie deserves to be blamed for something he did, then, as I understand free will, he has free will—or at least had it at some relevant time.

BOB: Why?

CLIFF: Because deserving to be blamed—morally speaking—and moral responsibility in general depend on free will.

BOB: Where are you going with this?

CLIFF: I can see saying that Ernie isn't morally responsible for anything he does because, in fact, Diana is morally responsible for everything Ernie does. After all, she built him to do it all, and her plan was foolproof. His doing it was an inevitable consequence of Diana's activity as his creator. If Ernie isn't morally responsible for anything, then maybe he has no free will. But what about Bernie? His story doesn't include someone else who is morally responsible for how he lives. So maybe he is morally responsible for some—or most, or all—of what he does. And if he is, then he has free will.

BOB: So you're saying that you've found an important difference between Ernie and Bernie—one that can explain how Bernie can have free will even though Ernie doesn't.

CLIFF: Yes. It's that Diana—and not Ernie—is morally responsible for what Ernie does, but Bernie—and no one else—is morally responsible for what Bernie does.

BOB: And then you say that because moral responsibility depends on free will, Bernie has free will even if Ernie doesn't.

CLIFF: Exactly.

ALICE: This is an interesting idea. But we can deal with it by adding something to Deb's story. Let's add that Diana is totally insane, no matter how brilliant she is. Let's also add that she has no grasp at all of morality; she doesn't know right from wrong. Then she's not morally responsible for anything, and we can't get Ernie off the moral hook by putting Diana on it.

CLIFF: I see. Back to the drawing board for me, I guess. But I still have the feeling that Bernie might have free will even if Ernie doesn't. I'll have to think about what, if anything, might justify this feeling . . . In fact, I'm starting to have a different feeling—that Ernie has free will too.

DEB: You'll get your feelings sorted out, Cliff. Don't worry.

ALICE: It's later than I thought. I'm going to head home soon.

BOB: Me too. I'll see you at the coffee shop tomorrow.

Alice and Bob say their goodbyes and depart. The others chat for a while before moving on.

3
Tuesday Afternoon

Scene: Alice and Bob are back in their favorite coffee shop.

ALICE: I think the others will be joining us soon. If they want to talk about free will, maybe we should move on to the mid-grade meaning. I'm sure there's a lot more to be said about regular free will, but it would be good to branch out before we return to the neuroscientists' claim that free will is an illusion.

BOB: Sounds like a good idea, and I'd say we're free to do that. Of course, we might wonder in what sense of "free."

Fran is approaching, followed by Deb, Cliff, and Ed.

FRAN: Hello dear friends. Are you talking about free will?

BOB: Hey, what happened to "Hi guys"?

FRAN: I wanted to surprise you with a new greeting.

BOB: And an elegant one at that.

ALICE: Bob and I thought we might move on to mid-grade free will, if that's OK with you guys.

CLIFF: That's fine with me. I'm still thinking about the Ernie and Bernie stories, but maybe we'll get back to regular free will later.

After agreeing on the suggested topic, Fran, Deb, and Cliff walk to the counter to order coffee. The other three friends chat about the sunny weather until they return.

BOB: Deb, can you give us a little refresher on mid-grade free will?

DEB: Sure. The basic idea is that you mix into regular free will what we called deep openness.

BOB: And what's that again?

DEB: A decision maker has deep openness when more than one option is open to her, given everything as it actually is just before she makes her decision. And "everything" means everything: all her thoughts and feelings, her brain, and her environment—not to mention the entire universe and its entire history.

BOB: Right, I remember. Someone who decided not to buy a coffee for me—Cliff, for example—might have decided to buy me one if he'd been in a better mood. But that's not deep openness. It's the kind of shallow openness you have if you might have done something different if things had been a bit different. In the wonderful language of possible worlds, you have deep openness only if you do one thing in one world and you do something else instead in another world in which everything is the same right up to the time you do it.

CLIFF: Wow! You're really catching on.

BOB: I hope I haven't been hypnotized.

DEB: Bob, when mid-grade free will came up last time, you said it brought to mind a brain flipping a coin or tossing dice, didn't you?

BOB: I did. I had a mental picture of dice inside a brain: one was blue and the other red. And there was a caption saying "This is your brain on deep openness."

DEB: Can you explain what's bothering you—aside from Cliff not buying you a coffee, that is?

BOB: Recall how Cliff linked free will to moral responsibility last night at the Warehouse. He said having free will is necessary for having moral responsibility—that is, for being someone who sometimes deserves blame or credit from a moral point of view. I think what bothers me is easier to see in terms of moral responsibility; and if I can get you to see the problem in that context, I can carry it over to free will.

ED: Sounds interesting; give it a shot.

BOB: I'll tell you a story about another guy named Bob. In his town, people do a lot of gambling. They bet on normal things like football games, but they also bet on things like what time the opening coin toss for a football game will happen. After Bob agreed to toss a coin at noon to start a high school football game, Cliff, a notorious gambler, offered him fifty dollars to wait until 12:02 to toss it . . .

CLIFF: Hey, you know I don't gamble.

BOB: It's another Cliff too. Another Bob and another Cliff.

CLIFF: OK. Sorry. Please continue.

BOB: Bob was uncertain about what to do, and he was still struggling with his dilemma as noon approached. He was tempted by the fifty dollars, but he also had moral qualms about helping Cliff cheat. He believed he should do what he agreed to do. Even so, at noon, he decided to toss the coin at 12:02 and to pretend to be searching for it in his pockets in the meantime.

CLIFF: Why did he decide to do that?

BOB: That part of the story comes a bit later. First, I want to ask a question. Keep in mind that mid-grade free will calls for deep openness. My question is whether Bob can deserve to be blamed for what he decided if he had deep openness at the time.

CLIFF: And what's your answer?

BOB: I'll get to that. Because Bob had deep openness at noon, there is another possible world with the same past up to noon and the same laws of nature in which, at noon, Bob does not decide to toss the coin at 12:02 and does something else instead. In some such worlds, Bob decides at noon to toss the coin straightaway. In others, he is still thinking at noon about what to do. There are lots of other candidates for apparent possibilities: at noon, Bob decides to hold on to the coin and to begin reciting "Invictus" straightaway; at noon, Bob decides to start doing jumping jacks straightaway while holding on to the coin; and so on. The candidates for apparent possibilities are genuine possibilities provided that Bob's doing these things at noon is compatible with the actual world's past up to noon and its laws of nature. The genuine possibilities are different possible *continuations* of the past.

CLIFF: You don't sound like yourself, Bob. Have you been hypnotized? But please continue. I feel like you're casting a spell over me.

Bob: Thanks. Imagine a genuinely indeterministic number generator. At five-minute intervals, consistently with the past up to that time and the laws of nature, it can generate any one of many numbers or no number at all. Its generating the number 17 at noon is one possible continuation of things, and the same is true of many other numbers. Imagine that, at noon today, the machine generated the number 31. If I verified that, I would believe these two things: the machine's generating the number 31 was a possible continuation of the past up to noon, and that continuation actually happened at noon.

Cliff: Those beliefs seem obvious.

Bob: Good. Now, if I were somehow to verify that, at noon, Bob decided to toss the coin at 12:02 and to pretend to be searching for it in his pockets in the meantime (*decided to cheat*, for short), I would have a parallel pair of beliefs: Bob's deciding to cheat was a possible continuation of the past up to noon, and that continuation actually happened at noon. Suppose Bob had deep openness at the time and another possible continuation was Bob's deciding at noon to toss the coin straightaway; in another world with the same past as the actual world up to noon and the same laws of nature, that is what happens.

Fran: I think I see where you're heading. As you know, unjust blame really bothers me. And I worry that the possible continuations of Bob's past are similar enough to possible continuations for the indeterministic number generator that whatever control Bob may have over whether he cheats or does something else instead falls short of what he needs for moral responsibility.

Bob: Yes, you do see where I'm heading.

Fran: Imagine a fleshed-out version of Bob's story in which although Bob does his very best to talk himself into doing the right thing and to bring it about that he doesn't cave in to temptation, he decides at noon to cheat. In another possible world with the same past up to noon and the same laws of nature, Bob's best was good enough: he decides at noon to toss the coin straightaway. That things can turn out so differently at noon—morally speaking—despite the fact that the worlds share the same past up to noon and the same laws of nature suggests to me that Bob lacks sufficient control over whether he makes the bad decision or does something else instead to be morally responsible for the decision he actually makes. After all, in doing his best, Bob did the best he could do to maximize the probability (before noon) that he would decide to do the right thing, and, even so, he decided to cheat. I'd say that what Bob decides is not sufficiently up to him for Bob to be morally responsible for making the decision he makes.

Bob: I couldn't have put it better myself, Fran. And here's the connection to free will. Mid-grade free will depends on deep openness. But deep openness at the time of a decision seems to bring with it something that poses a serious threat to moral responsibility. A person with deep openness seems not to have enough control over what he decides to deserve moral blame or credit for what he does. But if he really had free will, he would be morally responsible. So it looks like deep openness actually rules out free will.

Ed: That last part was a bit too quick for me.

Bob: Just the last part?

Ed: Yes, I see why you're worried that deep openness rules out moral responsibility.

Bob: OK. Here's a way to put it. Deep openness rules out Bob's moral responsibility for what he does only if it rules out his having free will at the time. Why? Because if Bob has free will at the time—well, actually, has it and uses it—he's morally responsible for cheating.

Fran: Right. If Bob freely decides to cheat, then he has no excuse: he deserves to be blamed for cheating. But it looks to Bob and me like he doesn't deserve to be blamed. So it looks to us like he doesn't freely decide to cheat—at least if free will depends on deep openness, as the mid-graders say.

Cliff: This is peculiar. You're talking as though the mid-graders are third graders—or maybe even kindergarteners. You're suggesting that something they say free will depends on—namely, deep openness—actually rules out free will.

Deb: Is that even possible? If X depends on Y, can Y rule out X?

Ed: Yes, it can, provided that X doesn't exist. Have you heard about the married bachelor society? They believe that there are men who are both married and bachelors at the same time.

Cliff: But that's crazy. Being a bachelor depends on being unmarried, and you can't be both unmarried (that is, not married to anyone) and married (that is, married to someone) at the same time.

ED: Excellently put. But if you tell that to the members of the MBS, they say because being a married bachelor *depends* on being both married and unmarried at the same time, being a married bachelor can't also be *ruled out* by it.

DEB: I see. I was wrong to suggest that if *X* depends on *Y*, *X* can't be ruled out by *Y*. After all, being a married bachelor depends on being married to someone while also being married to no one; and because that's impossible, it rules out married bachelors.

ED: Exactly.

DEB: But, Bob, are you saying that deep openness is impossible—like married bachelors?

BOB: No. I think it's possible, but I also suspect that it rules out free will—at least when it's involved in a person's decisions.

CLIFF: Are you saying that the mid-graders are making a simple mistake, as a third grader might?

BOB: No, again. Perhaps they haven't peered deeply enough into the very deepest depths of deep openness. Or maybe they think they can explain why deep openness doesn't preclude moral responsibility and free will. I'd love to see an explanation of that. It would ease my mind about mid-grade free will. The point I was making with the married bachelor society is just that even if we understand the meaning of "free will" to include a requirement of deep openness, as the mid-graders do, we can reasonably worry that that very requirement rules out free will.

ALICE: Is premium free will supposed to help solve Bob's problem?

DEB: I was wondering that too. We get mid-grade free will by mixing deep openness into regular free will—that is, into being a competent decision maker who makes informed decisions in the absence of manipulation and the like. And we get premium free will by mixing souls into mid-grade free will.

BOB: I don't see how that helps. If a totally physical person doesn't have enough control over what he decides in the presence of deep openness to be morally responsible for his decision and to make his decision freely, I don't see how adding a soul to the person helps. It's deep openness that poses the problem, not being totally physical.

ALICE: There are lots of religious people, of course. They believe in souls. I wonder if they—or most of them—think of free will in the premium way.

FRAN: I'm sure some of us are religious and believe in souls. I believe in souls, but I don't think souls are necessary for free will. They have other purposes.

DEB: That reminds me of a lecture I heard. It was partly on neuroscience, but part of it was about whether most people believe that free will depends on souls . . .

BOB: It would be nice if we had a short name for this soulful idea of free will. We have "mid-graders" for people who understand free will in the mid-grade way. What about "top-shelfers" for people who understand it in the premium way?

CLIFF: Excellent. And what about people who understand it in the regular way?

BOB: Reg . . . u . . . lar . . . istas. Regu . . . lar . . . istas. Regular. . . .

CLIFF: No, that's too hard to say—as you just now discovered.

BOB: True. How about "low-riders"?

CLIFF: Excellent again. So we have low-riders, mid-graders, and top-shelfers.

ALICE: Fine with me, but I'd like to hear about the lecture Deb mentioned.

DEB: I've been looking for it online. Here's something I found in the process, by a neurobiologist named Read Montague. It's from an article published in a journal called *Current Biology*: "Free will is the idea that we make choices and have thoughts independent of anything remotely resembling a physical process. Free will is the close cousin to the idea of the soul—the concept that 'you', your thoughts and feelings, derive from an entity that is separate and distinct from the physical mechanisms that make up your body. From this perspective, your choices are not caused by physical events, but instead emerge wholly formed from somewhere indescribable and outside the purview of physical descriptions. This implies that free will cannot have evolved by natural selection, as that would place it directly in a stream of causally connected events."

BOB: Wow! That's extreme. It's really out there. Do biologists think they have special insight into the meaning of "free will"?

CLIFF: I wonder how he thinks he knows what "free will" means. I can't see how by studying biology someone can figure out the meaning of "free will."

FRAN: Maybe the same is true of studying philosophy.

ALICE: Maybe. But at least philosophy has given us some options.

BOB: Right: low-riding, mid-grading, and top-shelfing.

ALICE: Deb, did you find that lecture?

DEB: No, but I think I remember it pretty well. It was by a philosophy professor who was presenting some evidence about how people think of free will.

BOB: Are you sure she wasn't a grad student?

DEB: He. And, yes, I'm pretty sure. He looked older than my dad even.

CLIFF: What kind of evidence?

DEB: It was a survey done with college students who hadn't studied free will.

BOB: Like most of us.

DEB: He had them read a little story. The first part went like this . . . In 2019, scientists finally prove that everything in the universe is physical and that what we refer to as "minds" are actually brains at work. They also show exactly where decisions and intentions are found in the brain and how they are caused. Our decisions are brain processes, and our intentions are brain states. Also, our decisions and intentions are caused by other brain processes.

ALICE: I see. If everything in the universe is physical and souls aren't physical, there aren't any souls—at least not in the universe.

DEB: Right. And the second part went like this . . . In 2009, John Jones saw a twenty-dollar bill fall from the pocket of the person walking in front of him. He considered returning it to the person, who didn't notice the bill fall, but he decided to keep it. Of course, given what scientists later discovered, John's decision was a brain process and it was caused by other brain processes.

BOB: And then what?

DEB: Then they were asked whether John had free will when he made his decision. Guess what they said?

CLIFF: Well, I'd say yes—at least if we're assuming that free will is possible. Maybe most people would.

DEB: Seventy-three percent of them said that John had free will at the time.

BOB: And the point is they're saying that even though they're thinking of John as a totally physical being.

FRAN: You have an amazing memory, Deb. Do you remember how many people were surveyed?

DEB: Ninety.

ED: Might it be that these people have really low standards for free will? Who were they anyway?

DEB: They were people right here in Tallahassee—students at FSU.

BOB: Hmm.

DEB: And about the low standards . . . The professor tried to get at that by having them read another story, in which John is under the influence of a "compliance drug" when he sees the bill fall. Only a small percentage said that he had free will in that story.

BOB: Well, at least the philosophy professor is providing some evidence about what people mean by free will. Dr. Montague seems just to be telling us what *he* means by it.

DEB: Right, I think that was part of the philosopher's point.

ALICE: We started on our latest track when I asked whether most religious people think of free will in the premium way—whether they're top-shelfers. If we did a survey of our own, I wouldn't be surprised to discover that most FSU students believe in souls. Fran said that although she believes in souls, she doesn't believe they're needed for free will. Maybe many FSU students are like Fran in that respect.

FRAN: Mentioning FSU reminds me that I have a paper to write.

ED: Not on free will, I hope.

FRAN: No, it's a paper on fruit flies for my biology class.

DEB: Remind me to tell you about a news article I read saying a team of scientists had demonstrated that fruit flies have free will. I can't do it now; I have to leave too.

BOB: How about resuming our discussion tonight? Warehouse at 10:00?

Bob's suggestion is unanimously approved.

4
Tuesday Night

Scene: The six friends are relaxing in the Warehouse. They've been talking about what place in town has the best beer selection and are swerving toward the topic of free will.

ALICE: What do you say? We've talked about various ways of thinking about what "free will" means. Should we move on to a scientific experiment or two?

BOB: How do scientists do experiments about free will, anyway?

FRAN: I've been looking into this. It seems that what got the ball rolling was some interesting work done in the early 1980s by a neurobiologist named Benjamin Libet.

BOB: Did you say Ribbit? Like the sound a cartoon frog makes?

FRAN: Libet; it rhymes with Ribbit.

BOB: I'm all ears.

FRAN: His main innovation was a method for timing conscious experiences that could then be correlated with measurable brain events.

DEB: What kind of experiences?

FRAN: Conscious experiences of urges, intentions, or decisions. Participants in the experiments were supposed to flex a wrist whenever they felt like it and then report a bit later on when they first became conscious of

28

their intention or urge to flex. They were watching a Libet clock. A spot revolves around the clock face in about two and a half seconds.

BOB: That's a fast clock.

FRAN: Absolutely. The participants were sitting in chairs, watching this fast clock, and flexing a wrist whenever they felt like it. Then, after they flexed, they reported their belief about where the spot was on the clock when they first became aware of their intention or urge. I saw a demonstration online. A bit after they flex, the clock stops moving and they move a cursor to mark the spot on the clock where they think it was when they first felt the urge to flex.

ED: What about the brain events? You mentioned correlating conscious experiences with brain events.

FRAN: Readings of electrical conductivity were taken from the scalp, using EEG technology. Brain activity involves measurable electricity—more in different places, depending on what part of the brain is most active. These days, participants in Libet-style experiments wear electrode caps.

ED: I see. I suppose everyone knows that "EEG" is short for "electroencephalogram." Think of a telegram, except that what does the writing is brain electricity.

FRAN: In order to get readable EEG, Libet's participants flexed at least forty times during each session. Readings were also taken from the wrist so that Libet could tell when muscle motion began during wrist flexes. At the beginning of muscle motion, you have what's called a "muscle burst."

DEB: So they flexed at least forty times whenever they felt like it and made a *consciousness* report after each flex. Electrical readings were taken from the scalp, and readings were taken from wrist muscles too. What did he discover?

FRAN: Well, there was already evidence of a progressive increase in brain activity before we make intentional movements. It's thought to arise from brain areas—toward the front of the brain—that prepare actions, and it's often measured using EEG. This increase is called a "readiness potential" or RP. One thing Libet discovered is that when he repeatedly reminded his participants not to plan their flexes in advance, he got EEG results that looked like readings for readiness potentials, and they started up about 550 milliseconds—a bit more than half a second—before the muscle started moving.

DEB: And what about the *consciousness* reports?

FRAN: On average, the time of first awareness of the urge, intention, or decision participants reported was about 200 milliseconds before the muscle burst.

BOB: So about one fifth of a second. And what is this supposed to prove?

FRAN: Libet's take on it is that the decision to flex right away is made unconsciously about half a second before the muscle moves, and so about a third of a second before the person becomes conscious of his or her decision. He believes that in order for free will to be involved in producing bodily actions, the decisions that cause these actions need to be made consciously. So he concludes that free will isn't playing a role here.

CLIFF: Just here or everywhere? Just in experiments like this or in all intentional actions?

FRAN: Libet suggests that we can generalize from his findings to all actions, and some scientists agree with him about that.

DEB: Let's see if I have it. Libet thinks that the decision to *flex now*—not just to flex sooner or later, or at some time or other—is made when the RP begins. That's about a half second before muscle motion begins. But because people's average time of first reported awareness of the decision is much closer to the time muscle motion begins—about a fifth of a second before it—he concludes that these people become conscious of their decisions to flex only after these decisions have actually been made . . .

ED: And because Libet thinks that to make a decision freely you need to make it consciously, he concludes that these people do not freely decide to flex and that free will isn't involved in producing their flexings. And he goes further: he suggests that we never make decisions consciously and that free will is never involved in producing actions.

FRAN: That's about it. But there's a wrinkle. Libet believes that once we become aware of our decisions or intentions to do something right away, we have about a tenth of a second to veto them; and he thinks free will might play a role in vetoing. As someone put it, Libet believes that although we don't have free will, we do have free won't.

BOB: Is that supposed to be funny?

FRAN: I guess someone thought so.

BOB: It would be nice to see a diagram of the RP.

FRAN: I made one. It's on my laptop. I'll show it to you.

Fran passes her laptop around. It displays the following diagram.

ALICE: I see at least a few problems with Libet's conclusions. For starters, why should we think that a decision is made when the EEG ramp-up begins rather than later? Maybe what's going on in the brain when the ramping begins is a process that might lead to a decision a bit later.

BOB: Is there a good correlation between the brain activity that Libet is measuring and muscle motion—the muscle burst—about half a second later? If so, I'm impressed.

FRAN: I looked into this. In these experiments, you use a signal to tell a computer to make a record of the preceding couple of seconds of electrical activity. The signal Libet used was the muscle burst.

ED: So then we don't know whether sometimes—even though the person didn't go on to flex—there was brain activity like what was going on in the participants a half second before they flexed. If you want to find out whether brain activity at a time is well correlated with an action at a later time, you need to look to see whether sometimes that brain activity happens and no corresponding action follows it. Call the first time "R," for "ramp-up begins." And call the later time we're talking about "$R+H$," for "R plus about a half second." You need to look to see whether it sometimes happens that there's a ramping-up at R but no flexing around $R+H$.

FRAN: Right, and Libet didn't look for this. Because of the setup, records of electrical activity were made only when there was muscle motion. So Alice might be right. What happens in Libet's experiment at time

R—or even *R* and the next couple hundred milliseconds – might be a potential cause of a flexing and a potential cause of a decision to flex. It may be a step along the way to a decision and something that sometimes or often doesn't result in a decision and doesn't result in a flexing.

BOB: I see what you mean. I sometimes take a step or two—or fifty—toward the library without making it all the way there.

ALICE: I also question our ability to generalize from Libet's findings in this unusual setting to all intentional actions. One day, I saw a video online in which a philosophy professor was talking about his experience as a participant in a Libet-style experiment. He said he waited for conscious urges to flex to pop up in him, so he'd have something to report when it was time to make the *consciousness* report. He waited until he was pretty sure the urges weren't just going to pop up on their own. At that point he decided that he would just say "now" to himself silently, flex in response to that little silent speech-act, and then, a little later, try to report where the hand was on the fast clock when he said "now."

BOB: Of course, he did this forty times or so to get readable EEG . . . Hey, I wonder how he decided when to say "now." Did he say "OK, now it's time to say 'now'"?

ALICE: He actually talked about that. He said he didn't know why he said "now" when he did. And that made me wonder . . .

BOB: Now I'm on the edge of my seat.

ALICE: In Libet's experiment, there's no reason to pick any moment to begin flexing over any nearby moment. It's like going to the supermarket, knowing that you're going to buy a twenty-six-ounce container of Morton salt . . .

BOB: For a tequila party?

ALICE: That's about as funny as *free won't*. Anyway, when you get to the Morton salt display, you just pick up one of those containers, and—ordinarily, anyway—you don't have any reason to prefer it to any of the nearby containers of the same kind. I wouldn't say that I use my free will in picking up the one I get rather than one of the others. But even if I do use it then, free will might work very differently when we're weighing up pros and cons and have to make a tough decision.

ED: I see, and that's why you wouldn't want to generalize from Libet's findings to all decisions—including decisions made after a careful weighing of pros and cons.

ALICE: That's right. There was no place for conscious reasoning about when to flex in Libet's experiment. As Fran mentioned, his participants were instructed to be spontaneous about their flexes. When we're working hard at weighing up pros and cons in order to make a decision about what to do, we're in a very different frame of mind.

BOB: Are you saying you accept Libet's claims about the wrist flexers then?

ALICE: No. I don't believe he's proved that they make decisions to flex before they're aware of those decisions. What I'm saying is *even if* he were right about the flexers, it would be a huge leap to the conclusion that *all* decisions are made unconsciously. Maybe when we consciously reason about what to do before we decide, we're much more likely to make our decisions consciously.

ED: How important do you think it is that we make decisions consciously? Sometimes when I'm thinking hard about what to do, I feel as though I'm getting close to making a certain decision. For example, I was accepted into three different universities, and I weighed up the pros and cons of each. I felt like I was really close to deciding on FSU, but I wanted to think about it some more. I did a bit more thinking, had that feeling again, and then just went with it—I decided on FSU. That's how it seemed to me, anyway.

BOB: I know what you mean.

ED: Imagine that when I had that feeling the second time, I unconsciously decided right then to go to FSU. Imagine that it took about half a second for me to be conscious of a decision I unconsciously made. Maybe consciousness is just a little slow to pick up on our decisions. If it is, would that mean we don't have free will?

BOB: I don't see why.

ED: Me neither. After all, I was doing a lot of conscious thinking in trying to figure out what to do. And it seems to me that my decision was a product or upshot of that conscious reasoning—my conscious weighing of pros and cons. If that's how it happened, the fact that I made my decision a few milliseconds before I think I did—if it really is a fact—doesn't make me worry about free will.

DEB: I see your point. Just like it takes some time for the sounds you're making to travel to my ears and register on my brain and in my consciousness, it might take a little time for our decisions to show up in consciousness. But it's not as though our conscious reasoning was out of the loop. The loop might just be a tad shorter than it seems.

ALICE: That's OK with me too, but are you saying consciousness of our decisions always lags a bit behind the actual decisions?

ED: Not me. I'm saying that *even if* that's what happens, it doesn't rule out free will.

FRAN: Do you mind if I backtrack a bit? Earlier, I mentioned Libet's idea that once we become conscious of our intentions, we can veto them.

BOB: Right, I remember.

FRAN: He even ran an experiment to test his veto hypothesis. He told the participants to prepare to flex at a certain time—for example, when the spot hits the nine o'clock point on the fast clock—but not to follow through, not to actually flex. And he took EEG readings.

BOB: Wait, you said he always used muscle motion to trigger the computer to make a record of the preceding brain activity. So how did he get EEG?

FRAN: You always need a trigger. In the main experiment that I described to you earlier, it was the beginning of muscle motion—the muscle burst. But in the veto study, the trigger was the spot's hitting the designated point on the clock—the nine o'clock point, say. He used the time as a trigger.

BOB: And what did he discover?

FRAN: Again, he averaged over many trials. What he discovered is that a ramp-up began about a second before the designated time and then petered out about 150 to 250 milliseconds before that time. Until it petered out, the EEG looked a lot like the EEG he found when people flexed at a time the experimenter selected in advance for them.

CLIFF: What did Libet make of this?

FRAN: He thought he found evidence of the power to veto intentions. He said the participants intended to flex at the nine o'clock point and then vetoed that intention. And he said that the part of the EEG before it petered out signified the presence of that intention.

CLIFF: There's something fishy going on here, but I can't quite put my finger on it.

ALICE: Maybe you did, Cliff, without being aware of it.

CLIFF: What?

ALICE: Let's try this . . . I'm going to count from one to three. What I want you to do is to prepare to snap your fingers when I get to three, but not actually snap them. Prepare to do it but don't do it. Ready?

BOB: OK.

ALICE: Bob, you haven't even put your fingers together in the way you need to if you're going to snap them.

BOB: But I'm not going to snap them. You said not to.

ALICE: Right. But I also asked you to *prepare* to snap them. If you don't even have them in a finger-snapping position, you're not preparing to snap them.

BOB: All right, I'm preparing now, and it looks like everyone else is too. At least their fingers are pressed together in the right way.

ALICE: Then here we go. One . . . two . . . three!

BOB: Right. No one snapped. No surprises there. We're all so obedient.

ALICE: And how many of you intended to snap?

CLIFF: No one, I'm sure. If we had intended to snap, we would have snapped. But what's the point?

ALICE: Two points actually. First, Libet's veto experiment doesn't prove that we have the power to veto our intentions, if his participants didn't intend to flex when the spot hit the nine o'clock point. And I bet they didn't. I bet they took the same approach as you in my little experiment. But the second point is more important.

BOB: I'm on the edge of my seat again.

ALICE: Recall that Libet got EEG in his veto experiment that—for a while, at least—looked like EEG in another experiment in which participants were instructed to flex at a preset time—say, the nine o'clock point again. So maybe in that other experiment, too, most of the EEG—or even the whole thing—isn't zeroing in on an intention. By thinking about our little finger experiment and the veto experiment itself, we can see that preparing to flex at the nine o'clock point isn't the same thing as intending to flex at that point. Maybe the EEG just picks up on preparing to do something, even when the person doesn't intend to do it—or, in fact, intends *not* to do it, as you intended not to snap your fingers. Maybe it picks up on imagining doing something at a particular time or thinking about doing something soon—or any of these things.

ED: I see. This fits with your earlier suggestion that maybe, in the main experiment, where the ramp-up starts about half a second before the muscle burst, the beginning bit of the EEG—or the first half of it or whatever—is correlated with something that precedes an intention rather than with an intention itself.

ALICE: Yes, it seems to fit.

ED: Do you think the intentions might not pop up in the main experiment until about 200 milliseconds before the muscle burst? As I recall, that's what Fran said was the average time that the participants picked out when they gave their *consciousness* reports.

ALICE: Oh, I don't know. Also, I wonder how accurate those *consciousness* reports are. And, as you mentioned, even if consciousness is a little slow in detecting our decisions or intentions, that doesn't seem to be a big problem for free will.

ED: Even so, I wonder how long it takes for an intention to flex a wrist now to produce a muscle burst. If Libet is right, it takes about half a second.

CLIFF: It would be nice to have a name for intentions to do things now. I suggest "proximal intentions."

BOB: Why "proximal"?

CLIFF: "Proximal" derives from a Latin word for "nearest" or "next."

ED: Sounds good to me. My question then is how long it takes a proximal intention to flex a wrist to generate a muscle burst.

FRAN: I read something that might be relevant. Whether it is depends on how intentions are involved in go-signal reaction time tasks.

BOB: What kind of task is that?

FRAN: In common go-signal experiments, scientists try to figure out how long it takes a person to respond to a signal with a predesignated action. For example, the go-signal might be the sounding of a tone and the predesignated action might be clicking a mouse button. Participants know what they're supposed to do when they hear the tone, and they're ready to do that. There's a warning signal indicating that a go-signal is coming pretty soon. The participants detect the signal and then click as soon as they can.

BOB: So they already intend to click the button before they hear the tone.

FRAN: You have to be careful now. When they hear the instructions and agree to participate, they have a kind of general intention to click the button whenever they hear the tone. That, of course, is different from a proximal intention to click the button—an intention to click it now.

BOB: I see. The general intention is something they have throughout the experiment. But if they have proximal intentions to click, they have many of them—one for each different click.

FRAN: Right. Maybe it works like this: the general intention—or even a more specific one like an intention to click the next time you hear the tone—in combination with your hearing the tone produces a proximal intention to click that in turn produces a clicking action.

ED: So you'd have a little causal chain in which a combination of things leads to a proximal intention to click, which in turn leads to a clicking. The combination is hearing the go-signal while having an intention to click the next time you hear the signal—or hearing the signal while having a general intention to click whenever you hear it.

FRAN: If that's how it works, you can get a pretty good idea about how long it takes an intention to generate a muscle burst. You can measure the muscle burst, just as Libet did. You'd know when the tone sounded, as long as you kept track. And since the proximal intention is a response to the tone, it would arise a bit later than the tone.

BOB: How much later?

FRAN: I don't know, exactly. But detecting the tone will take a little time. And if detecting the tone is part of what causes the proximal intention, that will take a little time too.

BOB: Got it. There will be a little time between the sounding of the tone and your hearing the tone, and a little more time between your hearing it and the onset of your intention.

FRAN: Libet's participants were watching a fast clock. So I looked for a go-signal reaction time study in which participants were watching a Libet clock. I found one. In it, the mean time between the go-signal and the muscle burst was 231 milliseconds.

ED: That looks like another piece of evidence that Libet is wrong to claim that the proximal intention arises around 550 milliseconds before the muscle burst. It's evidence that the time from proximal intention to muscle burst actually is less than 231 milliseconds.

CLIFF: But what if go-signals don't cause actions by causing proximal intentions? Fran described one way things might happen in go-signal tasks—a way that involves proximal intentions. But maybe things are different. Maybe something like an intention to click when the tone next sounds together with the sound of the tone produces a clicking action without producing a proximal intention to click. Maybe proximal intentions aren't part of the causal process.

ALICE: That does seem like a possibility. But it should make you wonder whether proximal intentions are at work in Libet's experiment. Here's an idea that parallels yours, Cliff. Recall that philosophy professor who said "now" to himself and then flexed. It seems like he had a general intention to flex whenever he said "now." His saying "now" sounds rather like a go-signal. So maybe he didn't have proximal intentions to flex either. Maybe his general intention together with his saying "now" produced a flexing action without producing a proximal intention to flex.

FRAN: Maybe so. And maybe something similar is true of other participants in Libet's experiment. Perhaps some of them use something else as a go-signal—for example, the feeling of an urge. If a general intention plus a go-signal can generate an action without working through a proximal intention, then this very point applies to any participants in Libet's experiment who use some mental event—saying "now," feeling an urge to flex, or whatever—as a go-signal.

DEB: I think I see where you're going with this. If it turns out that Libet's participants are using an urge as a go-signal and don't actually have proximal intentions to flex, then it's not true that the brain is producing unconscious proximal intentions. Proximal intentions aren't involved. On the other hand, if proximal intentions are involved, the go-signal information suggests they pop up much closer to the time of the muscle burst than Libet says—maybe around 200 milliseconds before the muscle burst, the average time participants later pick out as the point where they first became aware of their urge or whatever.

BOB: I feel an urge to relieve myself.

CLIFF: Will you use it as a go-signal?

BOB: Either that or I'll decide to go.

ALICE: I think some of us are getting restless.

DEB: Yes, I think it's about time to get going. But I do have a question. Libet's early experiments were done thirty years ago. We have much fancier technology now. Are there newer experiments that do a better job of proving what Libet thought he proved?

FRAN: I was going to look into that, but I ran out of time.

DEB: I have tomorrow morning free. I'll look into it then, and we can talk about it at the coffee shop tomorrow afternoon, if you like.

BOB: Excellent plan. I really need to go.

The friends call it a night and agree to reconvene at the coffee shop tomorrow afternoon.

5
Wednesday Afternoon

Scene: Deb is making some notes on her laptop in the coffee shop when the others walk in.

BOB: Have you been here long?

DEB: Longer than a few milliseconds, anyway.

BOB: How did the research go on new-wave Libet-style studies? Has newer technology been put to good use?

DEB: I found an experiment using fMRI and another one using depth electrodes. Although depth electrodes have been used since the 1950s, the technology is more sophisticated now.

ALICE: I know that fMRI stands for "functional magnetic resonance imaging" and it measures blood flow in the brain to see what parts of the brain have been most active in the past few seconds. But I don't know what depth electrodes are.

ED: People with severe epilepsy sometimes opt for a procedure that requires removing part of the skull. Electrodes are placed on the surface of the brain—and sometimes a bit beneath the surface—to identify places where seizures are generated so surgery can be performed on bits of the brain responsible for the seizures.

FRAN: Electrical recordings directly from the brain are much more informative than EEG, since the electricity measured by EEG has to travel through the thick bone of the skull.

DEB: Right. And if the patients wish, they can participate in various brain studies while the electrodes are in place, including Libet-style studies.

CLIFF: Cool.

DEB: Before I get into the studies and their results, I'd like to read you what a journalist said, based on her understanding of an fMRI study of free will.

CLIFF: Please do.

DEB: It's from an article in *ScienceNOW Daily News*. "Researchers have found patterns of brain activity that predict people's decisions up to 10 seconds before they're aware they've made a choice . . . The result was hard for some to stomach because it suggested that the unconscious brain calls the shots, making free will an illusory afterthought."

BOB: Sounds a bit like the Libet stuff, but with the predictive patterns showing up way earlier. Tell us about the experiment.

DEB: Participants were asked to make many simple decisions while their brain activity was measured using fMRI. The options were always two buttons . . .

BOB: Pressing one or pressing the other?

DEB: Right. And nothing hinged on which one was pressed—no reward, no penalty, nothing. The scientists say they found—and I'm quoting now—that "two brain regions encoded with high accuracy whether the subject was about to choose the left or right response prior to the conscious decision." They report that the "neural information . . . preceded the conscious motor decision by up to" ten seconds.

ALICE: Before we get into how this might bear on free will, can you tell us more about the study?

DEB: Absolutely. For one thing, the encoding accuracy in this study actually is only about sixty percent—fifty percent being chance, of course.

CLIFF: Really? Sixty percent? Simply by flipping a coin and basing my predictions on whether it comes up heads or tails—heads for the button on the right and tails for the button on the left—I can predict with fifty percent accuracy which button a participant will press next. And if the person agrees not to press a button for a minute (or an hour), I can make my predictions a minute (or an hour) in advance. I come out ten points worse in accuracy, but I win big on the matter of time.

DEB: Well put.

ALICE: What do you think the scientists are measuring or detecting several seconds before a button press? What is that neural activity associated with?

DEB: My bet is a slight unconscious bias toward a particular button on the next press. Possibly, the bias gives the participant about a sixty percent chance of pressing that button next.

BOB: What do you mean by a bias?

DEB: All I mean is that the person is slightly more disposed to press one button than the other next time. I'm not saying that the person feels the disposition or is aware of it. Put yourself in her shoes. You press one button or the other. You do this many times while trying not to fall into any particular pattern. So you're keeping track, perhaps only in a vague way, of your past button presses. And all this activity may give you a bit more of an unconscious inclination to go one way rather than the other next time.

ED: I see. These participants are like Alice in her salt example. When she goes to the salt display in the supermarket, she doesn't care which container she gets, as long as it's a twenty-six-ounce box of Morton salt. They're like the participants in Libet's experiment—except that they're picking a button to press for no particular reason instead of picking a moment to begin pressing for no particular reason.

BOB: Alice said she thought this kind of picking doesn't have much to do with free will and that, even if there is a connection to free will, it would be difficult to generalize from the findings in this sphere to claims about what happens when people have to make hard choices and are consciously reasoning about what to do.

ALICE: Yes, I did. You know, this time I'm reminded of a fable.

BOB: About salt?

ALICE: No, it's about Buridan's ass.

BOB: Whose ass? A fable about someone's ass?

ALICE: It's a donkey, Bob. And the donkey is hyper-rational, so it will never do a thing unless it has a better reason to do it than anything else.

One day, the ass was hungry and found itself midway between two equally large and equally attractive bales of hay.

Bob: I'm on the edge of my seat again.

Deb: Quit butting in, Bob.

Alice: The ass looked to the left and looked to the right. It had no reason to prefer either bale over the other, so it just stood there. Eventually, it starved to death.

Bob: I don't want to sound asinine, but I aspire to understand how this bears on the fMRI experiment we're talking about.

Alice: In that study, as in the Libet experiment, the participants are in a situation like the ass's situation. The solution is just to pick. If the ass had just picked a bale of hay, its story would have had a happy ending. And the participants in the fMRI study just pick a button to press—sometimes the one on the left, and sometimes the one on the right. Maybe this picking is an exercise of free will. We can call it "free picking." My concern is that free picking may not be very similar to free choosing in situations in which a lot of conscious weighing of reasons—pros and cons—goes into the choice.

Ed: OK. So we have the generalization problem again, as we had in last night's discussion of Libet's work. We also have the problem that a sixty percent accuracy rate in predicting which button a participant will press next doesn't seem to be much of a threat to free will. The prediction—made several seconds in advance of a press—might be based on brain activity that reflects a slight bias toward picking one button or the other on the next go. But slight biases certainly don't seem to rule out free will.

Bob: Does the depth electrode experiment go deeper, Deb?

Deb: In the experiment I read about, the researchers were able to predict something with eighty percent accuracy. The participants in this study are epilepsy patients who need brain surgery. Their task is to press a key whenever they want and then make a report after they press. They report their belief about where the hand was on a Libet clock when they first felt the urge to press the key. This is a belief about what the experimenters call "W time." That's what Libet called it. They're following him. With readings directly from neurons in the supplementary motor area of the brain, an area that seems to be involved in causing actions, the experimenters were able to predict what time participants would report. They were able to do this 700 milliseconds before the average reported W time.

ED: So seven-tenths of a second—a bit less than three quarters of a second. OK. Are you saying that eighty percent of the time, they were able to predict the exact W time that participants reported?

DEB: No, it wasn't that precise. Eighty percent of the time, significant changes in neural activity were detected about 700 milliseconds before the W time the participant later reported, and the W time predicted by the scientists was within a few hundred milliseconds of the W time the participants reported.

BOB: What is W time again?

DEB: It's the time at which a participant first becomes aware of an urge to press the key. The experimenters ask the participants to report on W time after they press the key.

CLIFF: Do the experimenters assume that these reports of W time are usually accurate?

DEB: Not really. They realize that the timing task is tricky. Just think about it. Participants are looking into their minds for an urge and trying to match up an urge popping up in consciousness with their perception of a clock hand that is moving very fast. I read an article about the difficult nature of timing tasks like these, but it's best not to get sidetracked by that issue now.

BOB: So what's the punch line?

DEB: Well, that pretty specific brain activity seems to lead to conscious urges to press the key. I mentioned that the recordings were done from the supplementary motor area, an area involved in the preparation and production of actions.

BOB: And how is that supposed to threaten free will?

DEB: The scientists who did this experiment don't make claims about free will in the article I read. But other people do see the results as being anti free will.

ED: Maybe people who see it that way are thinking that unconscious brain activity has already determined when the participants will press the key even before they become aware of their conscious urge to press it.

ALICE: I wouldn't be surprised if that's what they're thinking, and it's an idea worth considering.

FRAN: I see a couple of problems.

BOB: You've certainly been quiet. I almost forgot you were here.

FRAN: I know. I've been thinking . . .

BOB: Fran, before you tell us about the problems you see, I have a question for Deb. I understand what W time is and that the researchers are detecting some relevant brain activity about 700 milliseconds before the W time that participants report, but what is the time lag between this brain activity and the actual action—the key press?

DEB: The average reported W time preceded key presses by about 200 milliseconds. So the lag you're asking about is about 900 milliseconds.

BOB: Got it: 700 plus 200. Sorry, Fran. What problems did you have in mind?

FRAN: In the experiment by Libet that we talked about last night and the ones we've been talking about today, it seems like you're supposed to wait for an urge and then act on it. You're not supposed to plan in advance when to flex or click a key. And, in the fMRI experiment, you just pick a button to press, maybe in response to an urge. So we shouldn't expect the urges to arise out of conscious processes. But, of course, they don't just come out of the blue. That is, they have causes. So if the urges don't arise out of conscious processes, they arise out of unconscious ones.

BOB: I think I see. We shouldn't expect the urges to arise out of conscious processes, because the things they're urges to do aren't things that you have any particular reason to do. If the participants were consciously thinking about what to do or when to do it, then their urges—or at least intentions or decisions—might arise out of the conscious thinking.

CLIFF: When you say "conscious thinking" do you mean something spiritual or nonphysical?

BOB: No, I'm just talking about more brain activity—brain activity that is conscious thinking.

CLIFF: Got it. Fran, are you making that Buridan's ass point again?

FRAN: That's part of it. Even if urges are determined by unconscious brain activity when someone is simply waiting for an urge so she'll have something to report to an experimenter, an intention or decision might be caused partly by conscious reasoning when someone is thinking hard about what to do. Right, this is that generalization point again. But I wanted to make another point too.

BOB: Go for it.

FRAN: Ed suggested that the anti free willers might be thinking that unconscious brain activity *determines* the urges in this experiment. But given that the predictions are correct only eighty percent of the time, why should we think that determinism is involved? And even if determinism is involved, that itself doesn't bother low-riders about free will. Maybe I'm starting to ramble, but here's another point. If the participants had some reason not to act on an urge that they feel, maybe they could veto it. Maybe there's room for free will there. But in these experimental setups, there's no reason to veto urges. The participants simply wait for an urge to come along, so they can do what they're supposed to do: act on it, and then report a W time.

Bob: Hey, I think you were silent so long because you were keeping everything bottled up. It's pouring out now.

Fran: Yes, although I had a few urges to say what was on my mind, I decided it would be better to continue listening and thinking for a while.

Alice: All the points Fran just made are interesting. I'll just make one small point in reply. Libet says that some of the participants in his experiments reported that occasionally they had urges to flex and vetoed them. They said they then waited for another urge to come along before flexing.

Fran: That's interesting. It suggests that even if some urge is determined by unconscious brain processes, the process might not determine a corresponding action. By the way, if I were a participant in Libet's study, I might deal with the tedium by seeing what it felt like to veto an urge every once in a while.

Ed: I wonder whether I'd have conscious urges to flex. Maybe I'd be like that philosophy professor who just consciously said "now" to himself.

Fran: That's connected to another thing that was on my mind. In all the experiments we've been talking about, participants need to report on when they first became conscious of an urge, intention, or whatever. Maybe the main work for conscious experience to do in these experimental settings is to enable the participants to make their reports. What if people were told to flex whenever they feel like it while watching a Libet clock and were not asked to report anything?

Bob: Why would they be watching the clock? Wouldn't they wonder about that?

Fran: Oh, the experimenter can tell them that she's doing an eye tracking study or something while also studying wrist muscles. Here; I have a Libet clock on my laptop. I'll start it up. You watch it for two or three minutes and flex a few times. We can keep talking while you do this.

The six friends give Fran's task a try. George, a coffee shop employee, approaches them with a puzzled look on his face.

GEORGE: What's all this wrist action? Are you imitating a flock of weird birds?

BOB: We're doing a little experiment that Fran designed.

GEORGE: Hmm. It looks more like finger puppetry without the puppets.

BOB: I think Fran wants to know whether we had conscious proximal intentions or urges to flex before we flexed.

GEORGE: What?

BOB: Conscious urges or intentions to flex right then—just before we flexed.

George mumbles and gets back to work.

FRAN: Right. Did you? Did any of you have conscious proximal urges or intentions to flex?

ALICE: I don't think so, but maybe I was distracted.

DEB: I was paying attention to the clock and the conversation. I didn't notice any proximal urges.

BOB: I didn't either, but I was mainly imagining how weird George must think we are. That didn't keep me from flexing, however.

FRAN: OK. So imagine someone arguing like this: conscious intentions play no role at all in actually producing wrist flexes, button presses, or key presses in the experiments we've been discussing; so conscious intentions never play a role in producing actions.

BOB: Explain that first bit to me.

FRAN: What they're thinking is that you all did a lot of flexing in the absence—as far as you know—of any conscious proximal intentions to flex and that although conscious intentions are present in the studies we've been discussing, they're not needed to produce the actions. You didn't need conscious proximal intentions to flex in order to flex; and the idea is that the same goes for Libet's people. They're thinking that the flexings or whatever are produced the same way in both situations: the situation you were in, and the situation the experimental participants were in.

BOB: Got it.

FRAN: So back to the argument. I have two thoughts about it. First, maybe in these experiments conscious intentions are out of the action-producing loop. Second, it doesn't follow from this that they're also out of the loop when our conscious intentions are based on conscious reasoning about what to do. Here, again, we see a problem with generalizing from what happens in the experiments to a view about how actions are produced in very different situations.

ALICE: But suppose some of the participants use their conscious urges or whatever as go-signals.

BOB: Like the professor who might have used his conscious "now" as a go-signal.

ALICE: Right. That's the kind of thing I have in mind.

FRAN: In that case, the conscious urge or whatever is just as much in the loop as a go-signal is in the loop in a normal go-signal reaction time task. All I'm saying is that if conscious proximal intentions don't cause wrist flexes or button presses in the experiments we've discussed, we shouldn't conclude that conscious proximal intentions are never involved in action production.

ALICE: I see.

DEB: A while ago, Ed mentioned that some people might think unconscious brain activity has already determined when participants will press the key even before they become aware of their conscious urge to press it. When he said that, I started looking online for something about this, and I found an interesting thought experiment by a neuroscientist named V. S. Ramachandran. It's based on Libet's experiment.

BOB: Let's hear it.

DEB: We'll be backtracking a bit.

BOB: Fine with me, as long as we don't backtrack all the way to the ass.

DEB: I'll read the first bit to you: "I'm monitoring your EEG while you wiggle your finger . . . I will see a readiness potential a second before you act. But suppose I display the signal on a screen in front of you so that you can *see* your free will. Every time you are about to wiggle your finger, supposedly using your own free will, the machine will tell you a second in advance!"

BOB: Maybe I can put my finger on a problem with this.

ED: We'll see.

DEB: So now Ramachandran asks what you would experience, and he offers an answer. I'll read it to you: "There are three logical possibilities.

(1) You might experience a sudden loss of will, feeling that the machine is controlling you, that you are a mere puppet and that free will is just an illusion . . . (2) You might think that it does not change your sense of free will one iota, preferring to believe that the machine has some sort of spooky paranormal precognition by which it is able to predict your movements accurately. (3) You might . . . deny the evidence of your eyes and maintain that your sensation of will preceded the machine's signal."

BOB: Hey, I did put my finger on a problem. The scientist overlooked a very logical possibility. If it were me in the experiment, I'd want to test the machine's powers. I'd watch for the signal to appear on the screen and then see if I can keep from wiggling my finger.

ALICE: Libet's data definitely leave it open that you can do this. You might even display EEG that looks like the EEG in Libet's veto experiment. Maybe you thought of the possibility you mentioned because you realize something about a certain pair of statements.

BOB: Go for it. My mind is firing on all cylinders. My finger is on the trigger. What are the two statements?

ALICE: Here's the first one: "Whenever you wiggle your finger, signal S appears a second before you wiggle it." And here's the second: "Whenever signal S appears, you wiggle your finger a second later."

CLIFF: You're making my mind wiggle, Alice. I need to take a minute to think about these two statements.

BOB: Got it. The first statement doesn't entail the second. The second one might be false even if the first one is true. Here are two other statements for you, Cliff. First, whenever you win a lottery prize, somehow you acquired a ticket before you won—you bought it or found it or whatever. You can't win a lottery prize without a ticket, after all. Second, whenever you acquire a lottery ticket, you win a lottery prize. Obviously, the first statement doesn't entail the second one. If it did, I'd be rich. I can't win without first getting a ticket, but I can get a ticket without winning. Similarly, maybe I can't wiggle my finger unless signal S appears a bit earlier, but that doesn't mean that if the signal does appear I'll wiggle my finger.

FRAN: Absolutely. If Bob does succeed in keeping his finger still after he sees the signal, maybe the signal is a sign of the presence of a potential cause of a proximal intention or decision to wiggle his finger. Even when that potential cause is present, he might decide not to wiggle his finger and he might act accordingly.

ALICE: So Bob won't see the machine as controlling him. He won't be tempted to believe the machine has paranormal predictive powers. And he won't deny the evidence of his eyes.

BOB: Correct. I won't do any of the three possible things Ramachandran mentioned. I'll do a fourth possible thing—one he didn't mention.

DEB: The bottom line here, I guess, is that we haven't yet seen good evidence that our actions are all determined by unconscious brain activity even before we're conscious of any intention or decision to perform those actions.

ED: Sometime we should talk about how scientific studies bear on free will as the low-riders, mid-graders, and top-shelfers conceive of free will. Fran's remark earlier about compatibilism and determinism made me think this would be interesting.

ALICE: I agree, but it might be better to consider more scientific experiments first.

DEB: Yes, and something different might make for a nice change. Maybe we can move on from neuroscience to . . .

CLIFF: I've heard that there are some interesting experiments in social psychology that have to do with free will. Tell you what; it's my turn. I'll look into some of them before we meet next.

ED: I'll do the same. When should we meet?

BOB: How about my apartment around 10:00?

CLIFF: The Warehouse has more ambiance.

BOB: That depends on what you mean by "ambiance." But more important than ambiance, a serious storm is supposed to be blowing in from the Gulf tonight.

CLIFF: OK, Bob's place works for me.

General agreement. The friends depart.

6
Wednesday Night

Scene: Cliff and Ed are looking at their laptops in Bob's apartment while Bob tidies up. There's a knock at the door. Bob opens it.

BOB: Hi ladies! I thought Fran was coming with you.

ALICE: She's just behind us.

DEB: She went back to the car to get a book she brought.

CLIFF: I found some really interesting stuff in social psychology. It's about how people's behavior is strongly influenced by factors we might expect to have little impact on what we do.

ED: I ran across the same sort of thing, including an experiment in which participants thought they were giving extremely painful shocks to people. Apparently, they did it just because a man in a lab coat told them to.

Another knock. Cliff opens the door.

CLIFF: Come in, Fran. We just started talking about some psychology experiments we found.

FRAN: Hi. That was the plan, I know. But I was really hoping we could talk a bit about a recent book by Michael Gazzaniga. It's called *Who's in Charge? Free Will and the Science of the Brain.*

ED: Given the subtitle, I'd say he's a neuroscientist.

FRAN: That's true, but I read some social psychology too, and I think some parts of Gazzaniga's book sort of prepare the way for that.

BOB: Sure, Fran. Why not? You're in charge—unless Gazzaniga says no one is.

FRAN: Here's a quotation from the book: "When we set out to explain our actions, they are all post hoc explanations, using post hoc observations with no access to nonconscious processing."

BOB: "Post hoc" means "after the fact." It sounds like he's saying that we always invent explanations of our actions after we act on the basis of observations we make after we act. Can it really be true that we never succeed in explaining actions of ours partly in terms of *conscious* processing that preceded them?

DEB: That would be weird. We'd never have a good idea why we're going to do what we're about to do.

CLIFF: Right. And I thought I knew why I got up to open the door a little while ago—because Bob was busy and I wanted to let Fran in.

FRAN: I'm skeptical too. I read a review of Gazzaniga's book by a philosophy professor; I forget his name. He said he read the book on a flight to a conference in Munich.

BOB: Why is flying to Munich relevant?

CLIFF: Maybe he was making the point that the book doesn't take long to read, or doesn't require any more concentration than one can muster on an airplane, with all the commotion.

FRAN: There was more to it. He said people who invite philosophy professors to conferences don't pay for seats in first class. He likes extra leg room on planes. So right after he buys a ticket in coach online, he looks for an exit row seat—first on the aisle and then next to a window. If he finds a seat he likes, he snatches it up.

BOB: Sounds reasonable. But where's he going with this? Aside from Munich, that is.

FRAN: He goes on to say he does all this consciously and he doesn't know how to look for exit row seats unconsciously. And he says he does it because, at the time, he has a conscious preference for extra leg room on long flights and he knows—consciously knows—how to get the extra room without paying more than his hosts are willing to spend on a plane ticket.

Bob: I think I see where he's heading. He can explain why he looks for exit row seats in terms of something he's conscious of when he's doing that—wanting to have extra leg room, or his preference for the extra space.

Fran: Right.

Cliff: Why does Gazzaniga disagree?

Fran: Because of neuroscience experiments of the kind we already discussed—the fMRI study we talked about this afternoon and the Libet stuff. In response, the philosophy professor makes the generalization point we made ourselves—that it's a mistake to leap from what might happen in some special situations to a conclusion about all of our actions.

Bob: Maybe he has a time machine and was eavesdropping on us.

Fran: He points out that in the fMRI experiment, there is no reason to prefer either button over the other. So if the person were asked why he pressed the left button this time, he should say something like "I just randomly picked it, because I'm following your instructions." Because there's no place in the experiment for conscious reflection about which button to press; there's no place for an explanation of the button pressing in terms of conscious reasons for pressing it.

Ed: And the same general point applies to Libet's studies. His people are arbitrarily picking a moment to begin flexing a wrist. They're not supposed to reason about when to flex.

Fran: Right. But the professor says that when it comes to his selecting an exit row seat, things are very different. He knows he has a reason—a good one—to get a seat in an exit row rather than an ordinary seat in coach. And because he knows this, he consciously looks online for an open seat in an exit row. He adds that, given what he told us, we can predict with close to one hundred percent accuracy what he will try to do next time he buys a coach seat on a long flight; and, he points out, we get this degree of accuracy for free, just by consciously attending to what he wrote.

Cliff: I guess he's alluding to the expenses involved in fMRI experiments and the sixty percent accuracy in the study we discussed.

Deb: Sounds like it. But how does this connect to social psychology?

Cliff: I see the connection. Before you arrived, I mentioned to Ed and Bob that the social psych material I found was about how our behavior is strongly influenced by things other than conscious reasons. It sounds like Gazzaniga is getting at something like that from another angle.

FRAN: That's how I see it too. And now, Cliff and Ed, it's your turn to tell us what you discovered.

BOB: As I said, Fran's in charge. She's in a take-charge state of mind.

Bob hums a few bars from Billy Joel's "New York State of Mind" and then sings a verse.

BOB (*SINGING*): "I don't care if it's Chinatown or on Riverside. I don't have any reasons. I left them all behind. I'm in a New York state of mind."

CLIFF: I know what you're up to, Bob. I bet you looked into the social psych stuff too and found some experiments that are cited a lot as threats to free will. One is a bystander study that was motivated by what happened in New York City years ago when Kitty Genovese was stabbed to death in the middle of a street. Many people saw the attack. No one tried to stop it, and no one even called the police.

DEB: I remember reading about this in my Intro to Psychology course. It happened in Queens in 1964. According to newspaper reports, people witnessed the early morning attack from their apartment windows when they heard screams. But many of the details are disputed, including the number of witnesses.

CLIFF: I think Bob is trying to manipulate me into starting with a famous *bystander effect* experiment motivated by what happened to Kitty Genovese. He probably read about how we are unknowingly influenced by our situations; and by singing about New York—and singing a verse about leaving *reasons* behind—he's trying to pull Kitty and the bystander stuff to the forefront of my mind.

ED: That doesn't sound like the Bob we know and love.

BOB: Don't sell me short. In fact, I was one step ahead of you, Cliff. I figured that you'd guess what I was up to and then try not to be manipulated by me. I predicted that your response would be to start with one of the other experiments—anything but the experiment on the bystander effect. I was guessing you might go for something more upbeat, like the well-known study in which there's a huge effect on helping behavior when people find a dime in a phone booth.

CLIFF: There's no way to know whether you're continuing to try to manipulate me. I can't read your mind.

BOB: Maybe you can't read your own mind either. Maybe you don't know why you're going to start with whatever experiment you end up starting with.

CLIFF: I was planning to begin with the bystander effect until Bob did his manipulative musical act. But now I'm going to open with the Stanford prison experiment.

BOB: Because I guessed you'd start with the phone booth?

CLIFF: I don't know.

ALICE: Cliff, why not start in whatever way you think is most useful? Then, as long as Bob didn't influence your reasoning about the most useful way to start, you won't have to worry that he manipulated you into doing what you're going to do.

CLIFF: Good idea. Let me think about that.

BOB: I can see the gears turning in Cliff's head. I think his head is emitting steam. Or is it electricity?

ALICE: Leave Cliff alone. He's thinking.

CLIFF: I'll start with a famous experiment using nylon stockings. You'll see why in a few minutes, Alice.

ED: I see why already. I was going to talk about that study. Maybe I'll describe the Stanford prison experiment instead, if you don't mind, Cliff.

CLIFF: Fine with me. On to the stockings ... Shoppers were asked to say which of four pairs of nylon stockings were the best. The pairs of stockings were laid out next to one another, and they were of identical quality. The stockings on the far right were preferred to those on the far left by a factor of almost four to one. When asked about their reasons for thinking their preferred stockings were the best ones, no one mentioned the position of those stockings in the display.

DEB: Of course not. Everyone knows that where a pair of stockings is in a stocking display doesn't make it any better or worse. Presumably, they said the ones they picked were silkier or smoother or something of the sort.

CLIFF: And they were wrong. The stockings were identical in quality, and their position had a huge effect.

DEB: So what do you think is going on there?

BOB: It might be similar to a Buridan's ass phenomenon. The stockings are identical. They look at the left-most ones first, then the ones next to them, and so on; and they don't notice any difference. The ones they look at last *seem* best . . .

DEB: Why?

BOB: Because they haven't noticed any differences in quality, because they've been led to believe the stockings really do vary in quality, and because they're standing right in front of these stockings—the right-most ones—after having made some kind of assessment of the other three pairs. Of course, they don't realize that this is why these stockings seem best to them. So they invent reasons to support their assertion about the ones they picked.

ALICE: I see what Ed was talking about. The experimenters actually manipulated shoppers into believing the stockings on the right end are best. Interesting, and I see that there might be some connection to free will. But what connection do you see?

CLIFF: It's best to hold off on that question until we describe more of the studies.

BOB: Have you been manipulated into believing that?

CLIFF: I doubt it, and not by you anyway. OK, next in line is the phone booth study you mentioned.

FRAN: What happens? Does Clark Kent enter, followed by Superman's departure?

CLIFF: No, but it's almost as exciting. The researchers wanted to study the influence of mood on behavior—back when people used pay phones in phone booths and paid a dime for local calls. They'd even line up to use a phone.

BOB: Thanks for the lesson in ancient history.

CLIFF: Sometimes an experimenter would leave a dime in the coin return gizmo and sometimes she wouldn't. If she did leave a dime, she'd watch discreetly to see whether the next caller found it. The control group found nothing, of course—unless they deposited a quarter and received change. By the way, only people who checked the coin return were counted in the statistics.

DEB: And then?

CLIFF: The experimenter's sidekick waited at a distance for the people to complete their calls and leave the phone booth. Then she'd walk near the person and drop a folder full of papers in the person's path. She made it seem like an accident, of course. Also, the sidekick—or confederate, as they're called—didn't know whether the people had found a dime or not. Only the experimenter knew that.

DEB: That makes sense. If the confederate had known, that might have affected her behavior. She might have unknowingly tried to look pathetic or in need of help when she knew the person found the dime.

CLIFF: The results were amazing. Sixteen people found the dime in the coin return, and fourteen of them stopped to help. Twenty-five people did not get the dime, and only one of them stopped to help!

DEB: Wow! That is amazing. What a huge difference!

BOB (*SINGING AGAIN*): "I don't have any reasons. I left them all behind. I'm in a New ..."

CLIFF: Right, Bob. Finding a dime isn't a reason in favor of helping, and not finding a dime isn't a reason in favor of not helping. But the difference had a huge effect on behavior.

ALICE: Do you want to describe more experiments before we talk about connections to free will?

CLIFF: Yes, at least a couple. In the bystander study I mentioned, participants were led to believe they'd be talking about personal problems associated with being a college student. Each participant was in a room alone, thinking he or she was talking to other participants over a microphone. Sometimes participants were led to believe that there was only one other participant, sometimes that there were two others, and sometimes that there were five others. Actually, the other voices the participants heard were just recordings.

BOB: Not too exciting so far.

CLIFF: I'll get to the interesting part soon. Participants were told that while one person was talking, the microphone arrangement wouldn't let anyone else talk. At some point, the participant would hear a person say he felt like he was about to have a seizure. The experimenters call this person the "victim." The victim asks for help, rambles a bit, says he's afraid he might die, and so on. His voice is abruptly cut off after he talks for 125 seconds, just after he makes choking sounds.

Bob: So the participants who thought there was only one other partici-pant believed this other person was having a seizure. The ones who be-lieved there were two other participants thought that one of them was having a seizure and the other one was hearing it. And the ones who thought there were five other participants . . .

Cliff: You've got it. They thought one of the five was having a seizure and the other four could hear it.

Fran: So the idea is to see how long it takes for the participant to run out and get help and whether this depends on how many other people the participant thinks are in a position to help: no others, one other, or four others.

Cliff: Exactly. And here's what they found. Eight-five percent of the participants who thought only they could hear the victim's voice left the cubicle to help before the voice was cut off, and only thirty-one percent of the participants who thought four other people could hear the voice did that.

Fran: What about the people who thought one other person could hear the voice?

Cliff: Sixty-two percent of them went to get help before the voice was cut off. And there's more. All the participants who believed they alone knew about the seizure eventually reported the emergency, but only sixty-two percent of the participants in the "largest" group did this.

Bob: You said "eventually." So some participants reported the apparent seizure after the voice was cut off.

Fran: And the conclusion is that a person's belief about how many other people are around to help has a big effect on helping behavior.

Cliff: Right; that's the bystander effect.

Ed: Do you want to talk about any more studies, Cliff, before I describe the Stanford prison experiment?

Cliff: Just one more, I think. It's about helping behavior too. This one was done with seminary students. After some discussion, some of the students were told they really needed to hurry to give a short presenta-tion in a nearby building, others were told there was a bit of a hurry, and others were told they could take their time getting to the building for their presentation.

Deb: What were the presentations about? Or doesn't that matter?

CLIFF: Some were told to talk about the biblical passage in which a man helps another man by the side of the road.

FRAN: The good Samaritan?

CLIFF: Exactly. And others were told to speak about jobs that seminary students will enjoy most after they graduate and jobs they're best suited for.

DEB: OK. So they're testing to see whether the topic of the speech makes any difference and whether how much of a hurry they're in makes a difference. You said this study was about helping behavior. What's involved there?

CLIFF: On their way to the other building, the students pass a person slumped in a doorway. As they get close, the person coughs twice and groans.

DEB: The experimenters want to see which students stop to help, and maybe how much help they offer. Right?

CLIFF: Right. They developed a help scale that ranged from not even noticing the person in the doorway to refusing to leave him. But I'm not going to get into all that. There were forty participants. Forty percent of them offered some assistance—even if it was only as indirect as telling an experimenter's assistant about the person in the doorway. And here's the breakdown on being in a hurry. Sixty-three percent of the students who were in no hurry offered some help, and only ten percent of the students who were in a big hurry offered help. In the middle group, forty-five percent offered assistance.

DEB: So degree of hurry made a difference. And how about the topics of their presentations?

CLIFF: The experimenters say the topic didn't make a significant difference. So people who were actually on their way to talk about helping someone on the side of the road weren't significantly more likely to help than the others.

ALICE: I'm not sure this study shows as much about reasons for action as some of the others might. Maybe people in a big hurry thought it was more important to get to their presentation on time than to help the person in the doorway. After all, other people were likely to pass by and be able to help, but the student alone had the obligation to give the presentation—and, I suppose, to arrive on time.

CLIFF: Maybe so. These studies are supposed to demonstrate the effect a person's situation can have on his behavior. Sometimes, when people discuss the results, they focus on the difference between situations, on the one hand, and a person's character traits, on the other. And sometimes they focus on another difference: your situation versus your reasons for action. But in this experiment with seminary students, differences in the students' situations seem to result in differences in their reasons for action.

DEB: Right. A student who has no reason to hurry has less of a reason not to help the man in the doorway. And a student who thinks he has a reason to be in a big hurry has more of a reason not to stop. But it's probably more complicated than this.

CLIFF: It is. One thing that counted as helping was a student's simply mentioning that someone was in trouble when he got to the place where he was supposed to give his little speech. And people who were in a big hurry did that less often than the others. Reporting on the man in the doorway after they arrived for their speech obviously wouldn't have prevented them from being on time.

ALICE: I see. Is it time yet to make the connection to free will?

DEB: You sure are persistent, Alice. It's like when I was on a trip with my parents in the family van as a kid. My brother and I would keep asking, "Are we there yet?"

ED: It might be better to wait until we've discussed two other famous experiments—the Stanford prison experiment and a remarkable study of obedience that was inspired by Nazis.

FRAN: That's fine with me, but it's pretty late. Should we wait until tomorrow?

BOB: Good idea. I should get to sleep soon.

The friends chat about the family trips they took when they were children as they help Bob tidy up his apartment.

7
Thursday Afternoon

Scene: Back in the coffee shop. Ed and Cliff are ordering drinks at the counter. Bob sneaks up behind them.

BOB (*SINGING*): "I don't have any reasons. I left them all behind."

CLIFF: Still crooning? Have you seen the ladies?

BOB: They're chatting outside.

CLIFF: We'll get a table in the back.

Bob and the three women get drinks and join the others.

ALICE: It's your turn today, Ed. Are you going to start with the Stanford prison experiment?

ED: I decided to start with an even older experiment by Stanley Milgram. He wanted to understand why people obey commands to do horrible things they wouldn't do on their own.

BOB: Like some of the Nazi soldiers who worked in prison camps?

ED: Maybe so. Milgram's cover story for the participants was that he was conducting an experiment on how punishment is related to memory. They were forty men between the ages of twenty and fifty and from many different walks of life. Milgram worked at Yale, and the men were from that general area. They responded to a newspaper ad soliciting people to participate in an experiment on memory and learning.

DEB: What's the setup?

ED: The participant meets the experimenter and a confederate of his. The participant is told that he and the other man will draw slips of paper from a hat to see which of them will be the "teacher" and which the "learner." In fact, the participant is always the teacher. He hears the cover story and sees where the learner will sit during the experiment—in a chair where the teacher will supposedly administer an electric shock to him each time he gives an incorrect answer. The teacher watches the learner being strapped into the electric chair and is told the straps will prevent the learner from moving too much when he is being shocked.

BOB: Do participants actually believe the person will be shocked?

ED: They do. In fact, there's a video online. In one scene, a man who continued the shocks all the way through to the end is obviously extremely relieved when he's told at the end of the experiment that there were no shocks. And Milgram reports that, with a few exceptions, participants believed the setup was real.

DEB: You mentioned shocking all the way through to the end.

ED: Right. Participants are shown an array of thirty levers, each associated with different degrees of shock. The lowest shock is for the first incorrect answer, the second lowest is for the second wrong answer, and so on. Sets of levers—mainly sets of four—are labeled. About halfway through, the label is "intense shock," followed by "extreme intensity shock," "danger: severe shock," and finally "XXX."

DEB: Can the participant see the learner when he is being shocked?

ED: Not in the primary experiment, reported in a 1963 article. But in some other versions, yes. I'm starting with the primary version. If you like, I'll talk about some other versions a bit later. Also, in the primary experiment, the teacher doesn't hear the person in the electric chair speak. The learner answers by pressing a button. At one point during the experiment—when the shock level is pretty high—the learner pounds on the wall after being shocked, and from then on he doesn't answer any more questions.

BOB: How far along were they when the learner pounded on the wall?

ED: The learners had just received their twentieth shock. This was the fourth lever in the "intense shock" level. The shock levels were also labeled with voltage numbers. This one was 300 volts. Before shocking the learner, the teacher had to report the voltage of the shock he was about to administer: fifteen at the beginning all the way up to 450 at the end. At the beginning of the experiment, the scientist told the teacher, and I quote, "Although the shocks can be extremely painful, they cause no permanent tissue damage." When participants raised the issue of stopping the experiment, they were given stock replies ranging from "Please continue" to "You have no other choice, you *must* go on." The scientist started with a simple request to continue and eventually moved up to the "no choice" response if the participant persisted in talking about stopping.

FRAN: So what were the results?

ED: What would you predict?

FRAN: Well, you said the study is famous; so I'm guessing the results are pretty surprising.

ED: They are. As I mentioned, there were forty participants. Twenty-six continued shocking all the way to the end—even though the learner pounded on the wall after the twentieth shock and stopped responding to questions after that point. Teachers were told that no answer counted the same as a wrong answer.

BOB: Shocking!

ED: There's more. No participant stopped shocking before the twentieth shock. Five stopped right after that one. Four stopped after the next one: it was the first shock in the series labeled "extreme intensity shock" and the first shock in response to a non-answer. The other four dropped out a bit later.

DEB: How did the participants feel about this? Did Milgram say?

ED: He said they displayed enormous tension, fits of nervous laughter, twitching, stuttering, sweating, and the like. And when they talked about stopping, a calm reply by the experimenter often worked: "The experiment requires that you continue," "It is absolutely essential that you continue," or the like. If a participant refused to continue after being told he had no choice, the experiment was terminated and the participant was debriefed. This "no choice" response was the last in a series of four stock responses by the experimenter.

DEB: You mentioned other versions of the experiment.

ED: There were many other versions over the years. In one, the teacher could hear the learner but couldn't see him. The learner grunts in response to the seventy-five-volt shock and the slightly later ones. At 120 volts—labeled moderate—he shouts and says the shocks are becoming painful. He groans after the next shock, and refuses to continue in response to the one after that—the tenth shock.

BOB: So we're nowhere close to twenty yet, the shock that resulted in the learner pounding on the wall in the earlier experiment.

ED: Right. This goes on with increasing intensity for several more shocks. At 180 volts, the learner screams that he can't stand the pain. By 270 volts he's screaming in agony. At 300 volts—the twentieth shock—he desperately shouts that he won't provide any more answers. And he repeats this after the next shock—after emitting a violent scream. After all subsequent shocks, he shrieks in agony.

DEB: My goodness! Did any of the teachers persist to the end in this one?

ED: Yes, twenty-five of them did. There were forty in all. So over sixty percent of them went all the way. And in a version of the experiment in which the learner refers to his heart condition at 150, 195, and 330 volts, the results are about the same. Twenty-six of the forty teachers went all the way.

DEB: That's astounding! There's no way on earth I would do that.

ED: In two other versions of the experiment, the teacher was brought much closer to the learner, but everything else was basically the same— the groaning, screaming, and so on. There were forty participants in each. In one version—called "Proximity"—the teacher was just a foot and a half from the learner and could see him clearly. In the other—called "Touch-Proximity"—the learner could remove his hand from a shock plate in order to avoid being shocked, and the teacher would have to force the learner's hand onto the plate in order to shock him.

DEB: I'm not sure I want to hear the results.

ED: I'll tell you anyway. In the Proximity experiment, sixteen participants continued to the end; and in Proximity-Touch, twelve did.

DEB: How does this make you feel? I feel dismayed and disgusted.

BOB: I feel shocked.

FRAN: Can't you be serious, Bob?

BOB: OK. I feel hot, bothered, and . . . re-*volt*-ed.

ALICE: Maybe we should turn from feelings to free will. I guess the connection here has to do with personal control. Is what you do up to you, or is it up to your situation, so to speak? In these obedience experiments, taking on the role of a teacher in a scientific experiment seems to have a huge effect on the behavior of many participants. Maybe, to the extent to which this feature of their situation is effective, the participants aren't really in control of what they're doing. In fact, maybe the experimenter is controlling them.

BOB: That's interesting. Would you say something similar about the by-stander experiment—to the extent that their belief that there are other people around to help has an effect, they're not in control of their decisions?

CLIFF: Good question. That's the experiment with the faked seizure that I described last night.

ALICE: Maybe, Bob. I'm not sure. It's probably normal to be at least a little confused about what to do in a strange emergency situation like that. When they think that four other people are around to help, they might assume that one of them is likely to have a better grip on what to do about the apparent seizure.

FRAN: But the right thing to do is to run for help. They've got to know that, even if it takes them a little while to realize it. I recall that about seventy percent of the people who thought they were in the large group *didn't* do that—at least during the two minutes that they heard the frantic voice. I wouldn't conclude that they didn't have free will at the time or weren't free to run for help. I'd say they made a bad decision—and possibly made it freely.

ALICE: Tell me more. This is sounding reasonable.

FRAN: I think I want to put it this way: Believing four people are around to help makes it more difficult to make the right decision than believing no one else can help or only one other person can, but it doesn't make it impossible to make the right decision. I'd say the participants in this experiment aren't total victims of their situation. They're influenced but not determined by their situations.

ALICE: Would you say the same about Milgram's experiments?

FRAN: I would. But I still find the results surprising and disturbing. I also find it hard to believe that any of us would administer what we thought were very painful shocks just to help out in a scientist's learning experiment. But I have to admit that, looking at the statistics, I should believe that at least a couple of us would shock right up to the end.

Bob gets up, stands in front of Cliff, and stares intently at him.

CLIFF: Cut it out, Bob. You're more likely to be a shock man than I am.

ALICE: In light of the experiments in social psychology that we talked about, I believe that the situations or circumstances in which we find ourselves have a much greater effect on our behavior than I used to. But, like Fran, I don't see the situations investigated in these experiments as depriving people of free will entirely. My initial impression was hasty.

CLIFF: It seems that conversation and conscious reasoning can have an effect on Alice's opinions.

ED: I haven't described the Stanford prison experiment yet.

DEB: And no one has said what they thought about the phone booth experiment we talked about last night.

CLIFF: The results are truly amazing. Fourteen of the sixteen people who found a dime stopped to help; but of the twenty-five people who did not find a dime, only one person helped the woman pick up her fallen papers. Hey, maybe it was a magical dime! Did they use the same dime every time? Or did they control for individual dime power by using different dimes at different times?

BOB: Don't get carried away.

CLIFF: OK, back to earth. My hunch is that finding the dime boosted their mood and that people in better moods tend to be more helpful. Still, they help for a reason, the reason being that the woman needs help. Reasons aren't out of the loop. And this is true even if they would not have helped if their mood hadn't been boosted.

BOB: Fran talked about circumstances that make it harder to make the right decision. Maybe being in a good mood is a circumstance that makes it easier to decide to be helpful.

ALICE: Sounds reasonable. It might be time, Ed, to move from the uplifting to the depressing.

ED: You mentioned role playing in Milgram's experiments. Role playing is at the heart of the Stanford prison experiment. The experimenter, psychologist Philip Zimbardo, advertised in newspapers for male college students willing to take part in an experiment on prison life. There were seventy-five volunteers. After a lot of interviewing and diagnostic testing, twenty-four were selected. These guys were the ones deemed to be most stable and mature and the least antisocial. Three of them were selected to be replacements in case anyone had to leave the experiment early. Ten were assigned the role of prisoner and eleven the role of guard. The assignments were determined by coin flips.

DEB: Were they all students at Stanford?

ED: No, but all were staying in the Stanford area that summer—in 1971. In fact, the ones who were selected as prisoners were arrested at their residences, handcuffed, searched, and driven in a police car to a Palo Alto police station. From there, after being fingerprinted and placed in a detention cell for a while, they were driven to the mock prison built in the basement of the Stanford psychology building. When they arrived, they were stripped and sprayed with deodorant. Then, after being given a prison uniform and photographed, they were locked in cells. There were three small cells—six by nine feet—for the ten prisoners and a very small solitary confinement cell. There were also rooms for the guards. Much of the activity was videoed by hidden cameras. Concealed microphones picked up conversations.

DEB: How long did this go on?

ED: The plan was to do it for two weeks. The prisoners were there twenty-four hours a day. The guards worked eight-hour shifts and then went home. The guards wore guard uniforms, including mirrored sunglasses, and they carried police whistles and night sticks. The prisoners wore loose smocks, a nylon stocking cap, rubber sandals, and a chain that was locked to an ankle.

BOB: What was prison life like?

ED: Stressful and depressing. After the prisoners were settled in, the warden read rules they had to memorize. They had three simple, bland meals a day and the same number of supervised toilet visits. They walked to the toilet blindfolded and in handcuffs, by the way. They were also lined up three times each day to be counted. Prisoners were always referred to by a number worn on their uniform—never by their name. They had two hours of free time each day to write letters or read—unless that privilege was taken away. And they had chores to do—cleaning toilets and the like.

BOB: How did things turn out?

ED: I have a 1973 journal article by Zimbardo and coauthors on my laptop. Let me read you an amazing sentence: "five prisoners . . . had to be released because of extreme emotional depression, crying, rage and acute anxiety." Although the experiment was supposed to last two weeks, Zimbardo ended it after just six days. One prisoner had to be released after thirty-six hours. The reason—I'll read to you from a *New York Times* article about the experiment—was "extreme depression, disorganized thinking, uncontrollable crying and fits of rage." Another developed a psychosomatic rash.

DEB: How did they get to that point? What made things so bad?

ED: Several of the guards became bullies; and those who didn't turn mean just let the bullying continue. It increased each day. Counting of prisoners, which originally took ten minutes, sometimes went on for hours. During these counts, prisoners were encouraged to belittle each other. Over time, the prisoners' attitude toward one another reflected the guards' attitude toward them. Insults and threats escalated, and so did commands to do pointless or demeaning tasks. Guards sometimes made prisoners clean toilets with their bare hands . . .

BOB: Ugh. I'd just refuse. That's going too far.

ED: Pointless tasks included moving boxes back and forth from one closet to another and picking thorns out of blankets after guards had dragged the blankets through bushes. Sometimes prisoners would be made to do pushups while guards stepped on them. Guards would wake prisoners up in the middle of the night to count them. Sometimes they would deny them their scheduled leisure time just for the fun of it, or lock them in a solitary confinement cell for no good reason—a seven-foot-tall broom closet two feet wide and two feet deep. After the 10:00 p.m. lockup, prisoners often had to use buckets in their cells as toilets. On the second day of the experiment, prisoners staged a protest. The guards used a fire extinguisher to spray them, stripped them, and put the leaders in solitary confinement.

BOB: Ugh.

ED: The guards created a privilege cell to sow dissension among the prisoners. The good prisoners would use the cell and get better treatment, including better food. After a while, to confuse the prisoners, the ones who seemed worse got the privileges. Some of the guards became sadistic; and, of course, Zimbardo was as interested in the effects on the guards as the effects on the prisoners.

DEB: Did things get violent?

ED: There were some scuffles. But one thing Zimbardo insisted on when laying down the rules is that violence was strictly forbidden. The guards weren't allowed to use their power in this way.

ALICE: The theme of the power of situations is evident here.

ED: Absolutely. That's a major conclusion of the experiment. And bad effects of the situation showed up both in prisoners and in guards. The guards fell into three types. Some were tough but fair, some were good guys who did small favors for prisoners, and about a third were hostile and abusive. None of the testing the experimenters did in advance predicted which of the students would become power-loving guards. Some of the guards were disappointed that the experiment ended early; they were enjoying their power.

DEB: Doesn't this experiment seem cruel?

ED: It does, but one thing Zimbardo is trying to do is to make a point about the much greater cruelty involved in our prison system. If a mock prison has nasty effects on ordinary college students in just a few days, imagine the effects a real prison has. Zimbardo advocates prison reform.

ALICE: I agree that prison reform is a very important issue, but we're here to talk about free will. Here again, situations have a remarkable influence on people's behavior. I find what happens to the guards most interesting. I suppose I can see how an ordinary college student who has the power to do so might be tempted to make someone wash a toilet with his bare hands. But I can't see that the temptation would be irresistible. The guards who made people do this should have resisted the temptation, and I'm confident they could have resisted it. They were free to resist it, but they didn't. The guards' situation makes it easier for them to make bad decisions—decisions about how to use their newfound power. But I don't see that their situation *compels* them to act as they do. As I see it, it is still to some degree up to them whether they put their nasty ideas into action or not.

BOB: And what about the prisoners? Why would they do disgusting things they were commanded to do rather than refusing? Maybe they saw themselves as not being free to refuse. If I had been a prisoner in that experiment, I think I would just have told the guards that it's only an experiment after all and that they were going way too far.

ED: It is strange how people got sucked into their roles. Maybe we're not fully appreciating the power of situations. For example, during their free time, ninety percent of what the prisoners talked about had to do with their prison life. You'd think they'd prefer to talk about what they'll do when they get out—or their hobbies, their favorite sports teams, their friends, or whatever.

FRAN: Yes, that's strange.

ED: One of the prisoners felt sick and wanted to be released. He cried hysterically while talking with Zimbardo, in his role as prison superintendent, and a priest. After Zimbardo left the room to get the prisoner some food, the other prisoners began to chant that this one was a bad prisoner. When Zimbardo realized that the prisoner could hear this, he ran back into the room. Here's what happened next. It's online; I have a link on my laptop.

BOB: I'm on the edge of my seat.

ED: Zimbardo says: "I suggested we leave, but he refused. Through his tears, he said he could not leave because the others had labeled him a bad prisoner. Even though he was feeling sick, he wanted to go back and prove he was not a bad prisoner. At that point I said, 'Listen, you are not #819. You are [his name], and my name is Dr. Zimbardo. I am a psychologist, not a prison superintendent, and this is not a real prison. This is just an experiment, and those are students, not prisoners, just like you. Let's go.' He stopped crying suddenly, looked up at me like a small child awakened from a nightmare, and replied, 'OK, let's go.'"

DEB: Wow! He really was sucked in to his role.

ALICE: I agree. But suppose a guard had ordered him to shank one of the other prisoners.

FRAN: Shank?

BOB: Right, a prison word for "stab." A shank is a homemade knife. Alice must watch cop shows.

ALICE: Anyway, I bet he wouldn't do it. Something like that would bring him back to reality, just as Zimbardo's reminder about the real world did. My point is that the situation doesn't deprive him of free will. He can exit his role—even if his situation makes it difficult for him to exit it.

BOB: Are you sure about this, Alice? In Milgram's experiment, participants believe they were hurting the learner, and they did it anyway. Maybe a prisoner would have stabbed another prisoner if told to do so.

ALICE: You might be overlooking an important fact. Milgram's participants were told that although the shocks can be very painful, they don't cause any permanent tissue damage. But Zimbardo's prisoners know that stabbing someone would cause serious tissue damage. I don't think they'd do it. Even so, I wouldn't dismiss your point entirely.

FRAN: I've learned something important from all this. The situations in which we find ourselves do have a powerful influence on our behavior.

And now that I know this, it's something I'll keep in mind in my own life. You all know that I'm a bit of a nerd.

Bob: A *bit?*

Cliff: Come on, Bob.

Fran: I study a lot, and I care about my grades. I even try to get to bed at a reasonable hour so I can be well rested for my morning classes. When I'm at home, that's easy. But when I'm out having a good time . . .

Bob: Like talking about free will at the Warehouse?

Fran: Yes, actually. In that situation, even when I think I really should be going, I sometimes just go along with what everyone else is doing. I believe I should think more often about effects situations are having on me when I make decisions about what to do.

Deb: And that kind of thinking is certainly something we can all do. Our decisions aren't dictated by our situations independently of what we're thinking. Situations don't turn us into zombies or automata.

Alice: Maybe we should discuss what we learned from social psychology in light of the three different conceptions of free will that we talked about. I'm not saying we should do it now. Fran probably has to study; and so do I, for that matter.

Bob: I ran across another kind of argument against free will that also comes from social psychology. Maybe we can talk about that tonight before we go back to the free will gas station.

Fran: That sounds good to me. And can we start a little earlier than usual tonight?

The friends decide to meet at the Warehouse at 9:30.

8
Thursday Night

Scene: The friends have gathered in the Warehouse, as planned.

CLIFF: Hey, 9:35. I've never been here so early. I've never noticed those two old dudes shooting pool either. Tucker said they come here almost every week. They probably always clear out before 10:00.

FRAN: Maybe, like me, they try to get to bed at a reasonable hour.

ED: Right, that's why we're here so early. So, Bob, you were going to tell us about more experiments that bear on free will.

BOB: I'm ready. A social psychologist named Daniel Wegner wrote a book called *The Illusion of Conscious Will*. One of its main themes is that conscious intentions are never among the causes of corresponding actions. He regards that as ruling out free will.

CLIFF: On Tuesday night, Fran mentioned Libet's idea that in order for free will to be involved in producing bodily actions, the actions need to flow from conscious intentions to perform them. I guess Wegner has something like that in mind.

BOB: True.

DEB: I want to back up just one step. So my conscious intention to get here by 9:30 wasn't among the causes of my getting here by 9:30?

BOB: Right. But Wegner focuses on what we called *proximal* intentions, intentions to do things now.

CLIFF: I intend now to say "now" now.

BOB: You said "now" three times. Did you intend to do that?

CLIFF: And now I intend to snap my fingers now while ignoring your question.

ED: I heard you say "among the causes," Bob. That sounds a bit fancy.

BOB: Oh, that's not Wegner's way of talking. It's mine. Suppose I said that my conscious intention to be here by 9:30 caused me to arrive here by 9:30. That might suggest it was the only cause of this. But, of course, there were other causes. My car was working fine. I remembered the detour route from last time. My heart was functioning, oxygen was being carried to my brain, and so on. Also, I assume that my intention itself was caused by various brain events, by my remembering what we agreed to do, by my caring about doing what I agree to do, and a bunch of other things . . .

DEB: Including your concern for your friends. You're always so punctual. If you were late, we'd worry.

BOB: Absolutely. And I assume that causes of my intention are more remote causes of what my intention causes. I say "among the causes" to acknowledge all this. I suppose I could just say that my conscious intention was *a* cause of my getting here by 9:30. As long as you don't hear "*a* cause" as "*the* cause," things should be fine.

CLIFF: Understood. So tell us about Wegner's argument. You did say Wegner and not Vegner, right?

BOB: I did. He uses two kinds of argument for his illusion thesis about free will. One kind is based on Libet's work. Since we talked about Libet's experiments two nights ago, we don't need to go over that again. The other kind appeals to evidence of certain kinds of mistakes people make about actions and to evidence about automatic actions. I tried to figure out what kinds of experiments to start with . . .

DEB: And what did you decide?

BOB: I'll start with some experiments done in the late nineteenth century with an automatograph, a contraption that participants would place a hand on. There's a screen between the participant and a recording device that's attached to the automatograph. The device measures even tiny movements of the glass plate on the top of the automatograph.

CLIFF: Sounds old-school. Did you find a picture or diagram?

BOB: I did. I have it on my laptop.

Bob passes his laptop around. It displays the drawing below.

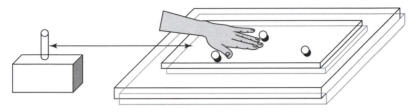

CLIFF: Cool.

BOB: Here are some of the discoveries. Suppose you had your hand on the contraption. If I started a metronome and asked you to count its clicks, you might unknowingly make tiny hand movements in time with the rhythm. If I asked you to think of the Warehouse parking lot that's now filled with rubble from the road work, you might slowly move your hand toward it—without knowing it. If I got you to hide something here in the pool hall earlier—a good pool cue, say—and asked you to think about the cue now, you might—without realizing it—very slowly move your hand in its direction.

ALICE: And why does this matter?

BOB: It's one piece of evidence that we sometimes perform actions that we're not conscious of and don't consciously intend. It's a small plank in an argument for the idea that conscious proximal intentions are never among the causes of corresponding actions.

ALICE: Let's see how it goes from here.

BOB: There's something called facilitated communication. It's a technique that was intended to help people with problems like severe autism or cerebral palsy communicate. Trained facilitators had the job of helping these people press keys on a keyboard—keys the clients were trying to press in order to type sentences.

DEB: How did they know which keys the clients were trying to press?

BOB: Facilitators were supposed to get a sense of which keys clients wanted to press by watching the clients' movements, and they were supposed to avoid controlling their clients' movements. They were there just to help the clients press the keys they believed the clients wanted to press. Many facilitators intended to do precisely this—just to help out and not guide or control. And they believed that was all they were doing. But it was discovered that these facilitators were actually unknowingly controlling what keys were being pressed and therefore what was being typed. The facilitators were the real authors of the sentences typed out on the keyboard.

FRAN: So this is another example of performing actions unknowingly that you don't consciously intend to perform.

BOB: Wegner discusses a spiritualist phenomenon called table turning. A group of people would put their hands on a table, hoping that spirits would move it. Sometimes, the table would move. The people were moving it, of course; but, apparently, without realizing they were, and without consciously intending to move it. This was popular in the nineteenth century.

CLIFF: I wonder if those two old pool shooters ever tried that.

FRAN: And now we have a third example of doing something without consciously intending to do it and without realizing that you're doing it. But how do we get from here to the conclusion that conscious intentions are *never* causes of corresponding actions?

CLIFF: Do you mean "never *the* causes" or "never *among* the causes"?

FRAN: I meant the latter. Sorry.

BOB: I'll get to that pretty soon, Fran. Here's something a bit different from Wegner's book. A certain kind of damage to the frontal lobes causes something called "utilization behavior." Here are some examples. If you have the disorder and I touch your hands with an empty glass and a pitcher of water, you might fill the glass with water. If I touch your hand with eyeglasses, you might put them on. And if I try the same thing with another pair of glasses, you might put them on right over the glasses you're wearing. Wegner suggests that the route to action here bypasses intention—that what happens is a kind of automatic response to a stimulus.

ED: That's similar to what happens in the experiments with the automatograph. There the stimuli are the clicks of the metronome and being asked to think about the parking lot or the pool cue you hid.

FRAN: And now ...

BOB: Yes, Fran, it's time to answer your question. I made some notes on my laptop about this. Here's a quotation from Wegner's book: "it has to be one way or the other. Either the automatisms are oddities against the general backdrop of conscious behavior causation in everyday life, or we must turn everything around quite radically and begin to think that behavior that occurs *with* a sense of will is somehow the odd case, an add-on to a more basic underlying system."

ED: I think I've got the idea. If it has to be one way or the other, then all my actions have to be caused in the same basic way. So if some of my actions are produced by automatic mechanisms rather than by conscious intentions, then all of them are.

BOB: Yes, that's the basic idea. Also, when we do have conscious intentions to do things that we do, Wegner thinks that we do not experience our conscious intentions causing our actions. Instead, he believes, we infer that they did. We experience our intentions and then, just a bit later, we experience our action, and we infer that the former caused the latter.

ALICE: Well, as far as I can tell, that inference might sometimes be right, as long as we're not inferring that the intention was the only cause of the action.

ED: The inference won't be right if all actions are caused in the same way—assuming we know that some actions aren't caused by conscious intentions.

DEB: And you have in mind the hand movements on the automatograph, the controlling actions by the facilitators, and the like.

ED: Right. I'm guessing Alice is willing to grant that these actions aren't caused by conscious intentions to perform them but unwilling to accept that all actions are caused in basically the same way.

ALICE: Exactly. I think some actions do have conscious intentions among their causes even if some other actions don't. I don't see why all actions have to be caused in the same way.

DEB: Is there any scientific evidence that conscious intentions sometimes are among the causes of corresponding actions?

BOB: I looked into that. Experiments on implementation intentions provide some evidence of this. The review articles I read aren't concerned with free will and aren't especially concerned with consciousness. But the results indicate that conscious intentions of a certain kind are remarkably effective.

ALICE: Tell us about it.

BOB: Implementation intentions are intentions to do a thing at a certain place and time or in a certain situation. I'll give you some examples from actual experiments. In one experiment, the participants were women who wanted to do a breast self-examination during the next month. The women were divided into two groups. There was only one difference in what they were told. One group was asked to decide during the experiment on a place and time to do the examination next month, and the other group wasn't. They wrote down what they decided before the experiment ended. And, of course, they were conscious of what they were writing down. They had conscious implementation intentions.

CLIFF: Why did you start with this experiment, Bob?

BOB: Not sure, and I'm certainly not aware of everything that influences my decisions. Anyway, the results of this experiment were interesting. All of the women given the implementation intention instruction did a breast exam the next month, and all but one of them did it at basically the time and place they decided on in advance. But only fifty-three percent of the other women did a breast exam the next month.

ALICE: That's remarkable. And it's something I should keep in mind myself. I should decide in advance on a place and time for my next exam. It sounds like that will significantly boost the probability that I'll actually do one next month. I often forget.

BOB: Here's another example. People were informed of the benefits of vigorous exercise. Again, there were two groups. One group was asked to decide during the experiment on a place and time for twenty minutes of exercise next week, and the other group wasn't given this instruction. Ninety-one percent of the implementation intention group exercised during next week, and only thirty-nine percent of the other group did.

ALICE: Something else for me to keep in mind.

CLIFF: Me too. I might even get myself into a regular exercise routine that way. After a while, I might develop a habit of exercising on, say, Mondays, Wednesdays, and Fridays before class.

BOB: One last example. This time, the participants were recovering drug addicts who would be looking for jobs soon. All of them were supposed to write résumés by the end of the day. One group was asked in the morning to decide on a place and time later in the day to do that. The other group was asked to decide on a place and time to eat lunch. None of the people in the second group wrote a résumé by the end of the day, but eighty percent of the first group did.

FRAN: Very impressive again.

BOB: And I've only given you three examples. In a review article I read, I learned that ninety-four independent tests of implementation intentions showed that they had a significant effect on behavior. And that article was published way back in 2006. I'm sure the number is much higher now.

ED: Conscious implementation intentions to do things certainly seem to make it more likely that you'll do them. All of the women in the control group had some motivation to do the breast exam; and many of them may have intended at the time to do one next month, but without consciously deciding in advance on a place and time. The implementation intentions certainly seem to be doing important causal work. But how important is it that they're *conscious* intentions? Would unconscious implementation intentions work just as well?

ALICE: That's a reasonable question. But what kind of experiment could be used to test the hypothesis that unconscious implementation intentions work as well as conscious ones? The experimenters would have to find a way to induce unconscious implementation intentions and then see whether they work as well as conscious ones.

CLIFF: How would they know whether they succeeded in inducing unconscious imps?

BOB: "Imps." Nice shorthand. Well, if they tried to induce them in, say, the breast self-exam situation and found that the women did significantly better than the control group, that would be evidence that they succeeded in inducing imps. But I don't know *how* they'd try to induce unconscious imps. Maybe hypnosis or something. They'd also need to check to see that the participants weren't conscious of the intentions they induced.

ALICE: I guess we'll have to wait and see. But at least when it comes to conscious imps, we have a good idea how they work. Presumably, in the three studies Bob mentioned, people consciously remember—at the right time—the intention they consciously reported earlier. And the fact that they consciously remember it increases the likelihood that they'll actually do the breast exam or the exercise routine or whatever. The conscious remembering would certainly help me. My main problem is forgetting.

DEB: I suppose someone might say it's the neural correlates of the conscious imps that do the real causal work rather than the conscious imps themselves. The idea isn't that unconscious imps are doing the work.

Rather, it's that neurochemical events are—the neurochemical events associated with conscious imps.

CLIFF: I wouldn't be surprised to hear that from some philosophy majors we know. The issue seems to be a metaphysical one. It's an issue for metaphysicians rather than for scientists.

BOB: OK. So the neural correlate of something like a conscious imp is the collection of tiny associated brain events, described in chemical or electrical terms or whatever. I think I see what you mean, Cliff. Sometimes I hear myself saying something stupid and, as it seems to me, that causes me to be embarrassed and to blush. Someone might say that it's not my hearing myself say something stupid, but rather the neural correlate of that, that caused the embarrassment and the blushing. This person might also say that my embarrassment itself isn't a cause of the blushing and that, in fact, the neural correlate of my embarrassment is doing the causal work. That's a metaphysical issue. If scientists can't actually separate a feeling of embarrassment from its neural correlate and see what happens when each one is present without the other one, they can't test to see which of them is doing the causal work.

CLIFF: Right. These issues definitely are interesting, but they're not scientific issues. Also, they're not crucial issues for free will. If the best metaphysical theory says that all causation happens at the level of subatomic particles, for example, so be it. Then, if we sometimes act freely, our free actions are caused at the level of subatomic particles.

ALICE: You're ignoring top-shelf free will. If free will depends on nonphysical souls or minds, it probably depends on those things doing some causing.

CLIFF: True. I was thinking about regular and mid-grade free will. Also, I have to say that, for all I know, the distinction between conscious implementation intentions and their neural correlates is artificial. Maybe the neural stuff and the conscious implementation intentions are the same thing. That is, maybe the conscious implementation intentions just are neural stuff.

ALICE: Is it time to see how the science we've talked about bears on these three different ideas of free will?

DEB: Alice, you're doing that "Are we there yet?" thing again.

FRAN: Before we do that, I'd like a little recap. As I understand it, one of Wegner's ideas is that having free will depends on your conscious intentions sometimes being causes—or, as Bob likes to put it, being among the causes—of corresponding actions. And another of his ideas is that conscious intentions never actually cause actions; instead, unconscious mechanisms do.

BOB: So far so good. And that second idea has two main parts. First, there's evidence that some of our actions aren't caused by conscious intentions. Second, all actions are caused in basically the same way.

ED: And when you put those two parts together, you get the conclusion that conscious intentions are never among the causes of corresponding actions.

ALICE: And this conclusion certainly is disputable. As I mentioned earlier, I don't see why all actions have to be caused in the same way. There seems to be a big difference between unknowingly moving your hand in the direction of an object you hid or toward the parking lot you're thinking about and intentionally leaving your apartment by 9:15 in order to show up at the Warehouse by 9:30, as you agreed you'd do. And Bob described evidence that conscious intentions sometimes are effective—that is, lead to the intended actions. If conscious intentions are sometimes among the causes of corresponding actions, then Wegner's threat to free will disappears.

FRAN: But you're not saying that it's enough for free will that your conscious intentions are sometimes among the causes of actions that you intend to perform.

ALICE: Right. Wegner says that something he regards as *necessary* for free will never happens. And I'm saying that the necessary thing sometimes does happen—that conscious intentions sometimes are among the causes of corresponding actions. But a necessary condition for something shouldn't be confused with a *sufficient* condition for it . . .

BOB: Absolutely. Sitting in a building is a necessary condition for sitting in the Warehouse—because, after all, the Warehouse is a building. But sitting in a building isn't a *sufficient* condition for sitting in the Warehouse. If it were, anytime we sat in a building we'd be sitting in the Warehouse. And, fortunately, most of the buildings we sit in aren't the Warehouse.

ED: Questions about what is sufficient for free will take us back to questions about what free will means.

CLIFF: Too true. And that was an excellent group recap. Now I think it's time for a nightcap. But not here. Let's go to my apartment. You can all walk home from there.

ED: Sounds like a plan. I, for one, consciously intend to drive to your house soon. And I expect to act accordingly. Shall we meet again tomorrow afternoon at the coffee shop?

DEB: Another excellent plan. I'm in favor of both.

FRAN: I'm going to head home now so I'll be well rested in the morning. I'll see you tomorrow.

The friends depart with conscious plans for the next hour or so and for tomorrow afternoon.

9
Friday Afternoon

Scene: The friends are seated by a window in the coffee shop.

DEB: Last night, Bob described scientific evidence that conscious intentions are sometimes among the causes of corresponding actions. Is there also scientific evidence that we have free will or that we sometimes act freely—in a "free will" sense of "freely"?

BOB: When we discussed implementation intentions—or imps, as Cliff called them—we had a clear idea of what we were talking about. Imps are intentions to do something—write a résumé, say—at a certain place and time. And scientists know how to conduct tests that provide evidence about cause-and-effect relationships. If the imp groups hadn't done any better than the control groups, that would have been evidence that imps don't have any more causal power than merely wanting or intending a goal. But things turned out quite differently.

FRAN: Right. If the group with the implementation intentions to do a breast self-exam at a certain place and time had about the same rate of actually doing a breast exam during the next month as women who intended to do one but who didn't pick a place and time in advance, that would have been evidence that the imps were no more powerful than simple goal intentions.

ALICE: There are some complications, as we mentioned last night. For example, it might be nice if someone found a way to induce unconscious imps in order to see whether or not they are as effective as conscious ones. And there is the metaphysical issue about whether imps or their neural correlates—or maybe both—do causal work. But that kind of metaphysical issue arises in many connections. When I looked outside my window this morning, I noticed that the street was wet. Was the cause the falling rain or the subatomic events associated with the falling rain? If you can't find a way to separate one from the other, you can't construct a scientific test to find the answer.

DEB: So, back to science, one thing that makes the question whether there is scientific evidence that we have free will difficult is the fact that there are various options about what "free will" means. We know what imps are—or what "implementation intention" means. But what does "free will" mean? We need an answer—or answers—to that question in order to know what we're looking for when we're looking for scientific evidence for or against the existence of free will.

ED: Or, at least, we need something like that. Suppose we know that X is a sufficient condition for having free will. Then if we find evidence that X exists, we have found evidence that free will exists. And suppose we know that Y is a necessary condition for free will. If we find evidence that Y doesn't exist, we have found evidence that free will doesn't exist.

ALICE: That takes us back to something I've been wanting to discuss with all of you. We talked about three different ways of understanding free will. We can discuss whether there is scientific evidence for or against the existence of free will as the low-riders conceive of it, as the mid-graders understand it, and as the top-shelfers think of it. And if we believe there is scientific evidence one way or the other about free will as understood in any of these three different ways, we can think about how strong the evidence is.

DEB: I think we may finally be there, Alice.

CLIFF: Me too. We made it, Alice! Shall we start with regular free will— the sort of thing the low-riders have in mind?

ED: That seems as good a place to start as any.

CLIFF: On Monday, we talked quite a bit about what low-riders—or compatibilists—mean by free will. So I suppose I can get by with a brief reminder . . .

DEB: Sure, and I'll even do it for you, if you like. According to low-riders, free will has to do with being a competent decision maker who hasn't been manipulated and isn't compelled or coerced. You're not hypnotized, no one is holding a gun to your head, and so on. You need to make up your mind about something, you're capable of making an informed decision about it, and you make one—on the basis of a consideration of reasons, or pros and cons. Satisfying all these conditions is sufficient for having freely made the decision you made.

FRAN: As I recall, low-riders aren't necessarily saying that all this is necessary for deciding freely.

BOB: Right. They're saying that it's sufficient for—enough for—deciding freely. Also, suppose you make a decision to vote *yes* right then on a certain proposal and that decision leads directly to your doing that—voting *yes*. Then, according to low-riders, you freely vote *yes* too. It's not as though what we do freely has to be limited to deciding freely.

ALICE: If the decision making the low-riders are talking about is *conscious* decision making, then one piece of alleged evidence that the sufficient condition they offer for free will doesn't exist comes from Libet's work and other neuroscientific experiments. Libet claimed, remember, that we make our decisions unconsciously and then become conscious of them about a third of a second later, and so do some other neuroscientists.

CLIFF: Yes, they say that. But on Tuesday night we saw that Libet's actual findings don't even support the claim that proximal decisions made in his experiment are made unconsciously. His assumption that decisions are made when the EEG starts ramping up is questionable at best.

FRAN: Right. And even if decisions are made unconsciously when there is nothing to reason consciously about, it's a long way from there to the conclusion that all decisions are made unconsciously—including all decisions preceded by careful, conscious reasoning about what to do. That's another point we made. In Libet's study, participants are instructed not to think in advance about when to perform the flexing actions, and they have no reason to prefer any moment to begin flexing over any nearby moment. Their situation is very different from the situation of people who are thinking hard—and consciously—about what to do. So even if the participants in Libet's experiment made their proximal decisions unconsciously, it would be a mistake to generalize from this to the conclusion that all decisions are made unconsciously. Maybe conscious reasoning about what to do significantly boosts the probability of consciously deciding what to do.

CLIFF: And as we saw on Wednesday afternoon, these same points apply to the new-wave Libet-style neuroscience experiments we discussed—the one using fMRI, for example.

ALICE: As far as I can see, the only other part of the compatibilist sufficient condition for free will that might seem to be called into question by scientific experiments we discussed is the one about being capable of making an informed decision. Someone might say that some of the experiments in social psychology that we talked about on Wednesday night and yesterday provide evidence that our decisions are too influenced by things that aren't reasons for action to count as informed decisions. Think of the coin in the phone booth, the experiment on the bystander effect, the nylon stocking study . . .

DEB: And the Stanford prison experiment, Milgram's shocking study of obedience, and the good Samaritan experiment.

ALICE: Yesterday afternoon, Fran made the point that although the manipulations in some of these studies—for example, Milgram's experiment or the bystander study—make it harder to do the right thing, they don't compel people to do the wrong thing and don't deprive them of free will. Now, Fran wasn't directly dealing with the question about informed decisions that I raised, but I think what she said bears on that question.

DEB: The worry now is that things that aren't reasons for action have too great an influence on our decisions for our decisions to be informed enough to be freely made. Assume that Fran is right and many decisions made in the experiments are free. Assume also that in order for a decision to be freely made it needs to be an informed decision. Then those decisions do count as informed enough to be free decisions—even if things that aren't reasons for action have an important influence on the decision makers. I have in mind, for example, decisions to shock the learner, not to go for help in the bystander experiment, or bully a prisoner in the prison experiment.

ED: Let's keep in mind that we're considering a proposed *sufficient* condition for deciding freely. So one possibility is that Fran is right in thinking that many of the decisions made in these experiments are free but, even so, they don't count as informed decisions. If being an informed decision is *necessary* for being a free decision, things are different. Then, if these decisions are free, they're informed decisions. But, be this as it may, we should consider whether the decisions at issue are free or not.

BOB: I agree. Deb made two assumptions to make her point. One of them is that Fran is right in thinking that lots of decisions made in the experiments are free. Maybe that assumption is correct. But we should think about it again.

FRAN: Let's go back to the bystander experiment. Even when the participants believe that there are four other people around to help, they have enough information to support a decision to run for help themselves. And you'll recall that thirty-one percent of the participants in this condition did exactly that. What the participants don't realize is how much influence their beliefs about how many potential helpers there are might have on what they end up deciding. But I don't see how this alone can prevent them from making an informed decision about what to do. Again, about a third of them do make the right decision, and I should think that many of the others were able to make the right decision too—given the information they had. In my opinion, probably all the decisions made by the participants were informed enough to be free.

DEB: And I assume you'd say the same kind of thing about the other studies.

FRAN: I would. In the Milgram experiments, for example, the participants don't appreciate the extent to which they can be influenced by the experimental setup and by encouragement from the experimenter to keep shocking the unfortunate learner. Nor do they appreciate how their earlier actions of shocking the learner might have resulted in a kind of psychological momentum that increases the probability that they'll continue to shock him. They don't have this information. But they have enough information to decide to quit.

ED: Also, I suppose that if you think some of the participants unfreely decided to continue shocking, you might point to the bit about manipulation in the low-riders' statement about free will. You might think that these participants were manipulated into deciding to administer extreme shocks to the learners in a way that made these decisions unfree.

FRAN: I suppose so. But I continue to believe that these decisions were free and that the manipulation wasn't so overpowering as to make them unfree. I'd say the same thing about the Stanford prison experiment. Alice made a nice point about it. Maybe she can remind us how she put it.

ALICE: It was about the guards making prisoners wash toilets with their bare hands.

Bob: Ugh again. Disgusting.

Alice: I said that although I could see how some of the student guards might have been tempted to do this, I couldn't believe the temptation was irresistible. These guards should have resisted the temptation, and I believe they could have resisted it. As I see it, they were free to resist it, but they didn't.

Deb: I remember. You also said that although the guards' situation made it easier for them to make bad decisions, you didn't regard their situation as *compelling* them to bully the prisoners. You said it was still to some degree up to them whether they acted on their nasty ideas or not.

Alice: I did. And I should say something now about the *informed decision* business.

Bob: I'm all ears.

Alice: I'm sure the guards didn't fully realize what effect playing the role of guards could have on them—how much it could influence their behavior. In this respect, they're like the participants in Milgram's study. But, even so, they had all the information they needed to make better decisions, and in my opinion, they could have made better decisions. I think their failure to realize how much of an effect their environment might have on them is compatible with their decisions being informed enough to be free.

Ed: In light of our reactions on Wednesday afternoon and yesterday to some of the other social psych experiments, I think Fran and Alice have said enough about the participants' information in the experiments they've been talking about for us to see what they would say about the other experiments.

Deb: The hypothesis on the table now is that things that aren't reasons for action have too great an influence on our decisions for our decisions to be informed enough to be freely made.

Ed: Right. And Fran and Alice are saying that the participants in the experiments have enough information to make free decisions.

Cliff: I agree with them. I also like a point Ed made earlier. If you think these participants aren't making free decisions, that might be because you're thinking that the experimental manipulations prevent them from deciding freely. But the low-riders have that covered. The sufficient condition for free deciding that they offer includes the condition that the decider hasn't been manipulated.

BOB: True. They don't say that not being manipulated is *necessary* for deciding freely. So they can agree with Alice and Fran that the manipulated participants are deciding freely. But if you refuse to accept that about some of the decisions—say, some decisions to administer the maximum shock—the low-riders can say that even if you're right to claim that these decisions are unfree, that's because the power of the manipulation is too great.

ED: And, of course, there are times when we aren't being manipulated at all. Even if heavy-duty manipulation rules out free will, it certainly doesn't follow that we never decide freely.

ALICE: That point may seem obvious, but it's important. People shouldn't generalize from what's true in cases of extreme manipulation to a judgment about what's true in all cases—including cases in which there's no manipulation at all.

BOB: One thing we asked is whether there's evidence that we sometimes do decide freely, assuming the low-riders have the lowdown on what "free will" means. I'm curious what all of you think about this.

CLIFF: Thanks for bringing us back to this, Bob. Again, the conditions the low-riders offer as sufficient for deciding freely are these: being a competent decision maker who hasn't been manipulated (in some way relevant to what decision you make, of course) and isn't being compelled or coerced; being capable of making an informed decision about the matter at hand; and making an informed decision on the basis of reasons.

ALICE: And there's lots of evidence that people sometimes satisfy all of these conditions. There is evidence that we sometimes make informed decisions on the basis of a consideration of pros and cons. Just think about many of the decisions we've made in the course of our discussion of free will—our decision to meet at the Warehouse at 9:30 last night, Cliff's decision to start with the nylon stocking experiment Wednesday night, Fran's decision not to join us for the nightcap last night, and so on. They were informed decisions. And we have evidence that they were: they made good sense in light of the information we had. Also, we have grounds for believing that these decisions weren't coerced, weren't compelled, and weren't products of manipulation.

BOB: What grounds do you have in mind?

ALICE: The combination of two things: first, our experience of reasoning about what to do and deciding on the basis of our reasoning; and second, the absence of any reason to believe we were being coerced, compelled, or manipulated. We certainly felt like none of this was happening to us; that's part of our experience of reasoning and deciding in normal situations. And we don't have any reason to believe that our feelings about this were off target.

BOB: Got it. So if "free will" means what low-riders say it does, we have evidence that people sometimes make free decisions.

ALICE: Right.

FRAN: But if low-riders are wrong about what free will means, we need to go further.

ED: True. I noticed something relevant to this when Fran and Alice were talking about the social psych experiments. Several times they said participants could have acted differently than they did. Do you recall our discussion on Monday afternoon of "could have"?

CLIFF: Yes, as some compatibilists think about it, the fact that someone could have made a different decision than he did is compatible with determinism. Even if determinism is true, they say, you might have acted differently if things had been a bit different—say, if your mood had been a bit different or if you had thought about things just a bit more. But as mid-graders tend to think about it, having been able to do otherwise depends on deep openness.

BOB: Ah, yes, the abyss: the deepest depths of deep openness.

DEB: What you need for deep openness is that more than one option was open to you, given everything as it actually was at the time—your mood, all your thoughts and feelings, your brain, your environment, and, indeed, the entire universe and its entire history.

BOB: I have the feeling you said this exactly the same way on Monday. You do have an amazing memory.

ED: And I remember, Deb, that you wanted to tell us something about fruit flies.

DEB: It was about a news article I read saying a team of scientists had found free will in fruit flies. Actually, the experiment was about whether the tiny fly brain works deterministically or indeterministically. I can put the issue in terms of possible worlds—something we talked about Monday afternoon. Suppose a fly turns to the right at a particular time. Is there another possible world in which absolutely everything is the same up until then and it does something else instead? If these scientists are right, the answer is yes.

CLIFF: Of course, that doesn't mean that flies have free will. An animal can do something unfreely while having been able to do something else unfreely.

DEB: Absolutely. What's interesting is that animal brains might be indeterministic organs. We're animals, of course. And if our brains are indeterministic, maybe we sometimes have deep openness.

ED: We seem to have moved on to free will as the mid-graders think of it. Maybe Deb can remind us what they have in mind.

DEB: The basic idea is that mid-graders add deep openness to the low-riders' idea of free will. Think about a competent decision maker who hasn't been manipulated and isn't being compelled or coerced and mix in deep openness. If the person makes an informed decision, and if he could have made a different decision right then, he has free will at the time—as mid-graders think of free will.

ED: OK. The experiments we've discussed don't rule out the existence of low-rider free will. So the only way for them to rule out the existence of mid-grade free will is to prove that this extra element—deep openness—doesn't exist.

ALICE: Right. Let's say that low-riding free will is X plus Y plus Z. Then mid-grade free will is X plus Y plus Z plus deep openness. So if the results of the experiments are compatible with the existence of low-riding free will, then they're compatible with everything in mid-grade free will except possibly deep openness.

BOB: So do any of the experiments rule out deep openness?

ED: I suppose someone might think the neuroscience experiments we talked about provide evidence that the brain works deterministically. But, of course, they don't. The most impressive success rate we found at predicting what a participant would do on the basis of brain readings was eighty percent. This was the one using depth electrodes. From brain readings, the experimenters could predict with eighty percent accuracy roughly what time participants would report as their W time. W time, remember, is the time they say they first felt the proximal urge or intention to move. Here we have probabilities. So we have something that's compatible with the brain *not* working deterministically—with there being some wiggle room in the brain.

BOB: Do you think that if the technology were better, the success rate of predictions might go all the way up to one hundred percent?

ED: I'll believe that when I see it. And don't forget what Deb told us about the fruit flies. Some scientists interpret their findings as evidence that fly brains are indeterministic organs. If they're right, brain indeterminism might be part of our evolutionary heritage.

BOB: But is there positive evidence our brains work indeterministically in the way they'd need to if we have deep openness? Is there evidence that sometimes, right up to the moment of decision, there really are different possibilities for what happens next in the brain?

DEB: I looked for such evidence, and the best I could do was the fruit fly experiment. But, of course, human brains are enormously complicated. It would be extremely difficult—and certainly not possible today—to control everything so you could tell that a brain event wasn't determined by anything and was partly a matter of chance.

BOB: Think about hearing the click of a Geiger counter. If my physics friends are right, those clicks are caused by something that's not deterministically caused—beta decay.

ALICE: Is it important to know what beta decay is for our purposes?

BOB: Not really. But it's a kind of radioactive decay. It happens when an atom emits an electron or a positron. My physics friends tell me that this process is not deterministic—that the laws that govern it are just probabilistic. A particular atom may or may not emit a beta particle—that is, an electron or a positron—at a given time. Whether it happens or not at the time isn't settled in advance, or so they say. And my point was that, if they're right, then some undetermined events might cause things we can detect—like clicks of a Geiger counter.

DEB: Suppose that's right about what happens out there in the world. How do we know that once the sound waves hit the eardrums things don't go all deterministic in the brain?

BOB: I see. But we don't know that things *do* go all deterministic either, right?

DEB: Right. As far as I can tell, we don't have good evidence that the brain works deterministically and we don't have good evidence that it works indeterministically in ways it would need to if we have mid-grade free will.

BOB: But it does feel like we could have decided differently. Sometimes I have that very feeling when I decide. Isn't that evidence of deep openness?

ALICE: Imagine that tomorrow we read in the newspaper that physicists had an enormous breakthrough. They proved determinism is true. Would you know the news is wrong just on the basis of your own personal experience?

ED: How do you think things would feel if determinism were true?

BOB: Just the way they do now, I suppose. I see the point, Ed.

CLIFF: I think I just saw Sally across the street. I'm going to run out and check.

Cliff rushes out of the coffee shop. The friends watch him through the window.

DEB: That would be excellent timing. I have the feeling we'll be turning to premium free will soon. It would be good to have our most spiritual friend here for that.

Cliff returns.

CLIFF: Whoever it was seems to have vanished into thin air.

BOB: Maybe it *was* Sally then.

ALICE: I know it's Friday and you might have other things to do tonight, but if not . . .

FRAN: Let me predict the rest of the sentence: Would you like to meet tonight to talk about free will?

ALICE: I don't know whether those would have been my exact words or not, but that's the basic idea.

BOB: I feel like if I say yes, I'll be admitting I've become a nerd.

ED: There's absolutely nothing wrong with being a nerd, Bob.

FRAN: Right. Join the crowd.

CLIFF: I'd like to make an informed decision about what to do tonight. So I'll reflect a bit.

DEB: 10:00 at the Warehouse then?

CLIFF: Sure. Why not?

Everyone happily agrees, and the friends go their separate ways.

10

Friday Night

Scene: The friends are soaking in the Warehouse ambiance. It's raining lightly.

CLIFF: I invited Sally to join us, but I forgot to tell her about the detour. I wonder when the road work will be finished.

FRAN: It will be good to see her. You know, we've covered a lot of ground this week. We won't have time to bring her up to speed on free will.

CLIFF: I thought about that—for quite a while, actually.

BOB: Consciously or unconsciously?

CLIFF: Well, I know I did a lot of conscious thinking about it. If I thought about it unconsciously too, I have no way of knowing how long that went on.

FRAN: Tell us about your conscious thinking.

CLIFF: I believed Sally would be useful as a consultant about what makes premium free will different—that is, a nonphysical soul or mind. I also believed she'd like the topic of free will, even without all the background. In fact, I gave her a little background on free will, and I asked her whether she might find a discussion of premium free will interesting. She said she would. So, on the whole, I deemed inviting her an excellent idea. Therefore, I decided to do that.

BOB: Extremely thoughtful, Cliff. But did you decide consciously or unconsciously?

CLIFF: Consciously, I think. But perhaps my conscious thinking resulted in an unconscious decision that I became conscious of a few milliseconds later.

BOB: A few milliseconds after you invited her?

CLIFF: No, a few milliseconds after I unconsciously made the decision. It took me a while to find my phone and make the call.

ALICE: Maybe you guys should get that topic out of your systems before Sally arrives. Explaining all that neuroscience to her might take us off track.

Sally arrives. As she walks in, the ancient Warehouse air conditioner starts up and the lights flicker, go off entirely for a couple of seconds, and come back on.

BOB: Last month, after a couple of flickers like that, the power in the whole building went down for about twenty minutes. I hope we're not in for that again.

ED: What a dramatic entry, Sally! Great to see you!

SALLY: Hi guys. I hear you've become very philosophical. Have you started looking into crystal therapy, astral projection, and that sort of thing? Or are you talking about the kind of philosophy that philosophy professors talk about?

ED: The latter—especially free will. And we've chatted quite a bit about some scientific experiments and how they might bear on free will. Our plan for tonight—at least at the beginning—is to talk about a spiritual way of thinking about free will and what science might tell us about free will when we think of it that way.

SALLY: Sounds fascinating. Tell me more.

FRAN: We've been using a gas station analogy. Three kinds of gas— regular, mid-grade, and premium—and three ways of understanding free will. In each case, we concentrate on what would be sufficient for having free will—or sufficient for making a decision freely, as we say.

SALLY: Sufficient, you say. So even in the case of just one particular grade of free will, you're not trying to find precise boundaries. You're not looking for a set of necessary conditions for free will that add up to a sufficient condition for it. Is that right?

ALICE: Right. That would be a difficult project with any of the three grades. Patrolling the border of some concepts is hard work. There often are lots of borderline cases to consider—or at least what might look like borderline cases. If parts of the sufficient conditions we consider aren't necessary for free will, that's OK with us.

CLIFF: Here's a way to think about it, Sally. Imagine there's no good scientific evidence that people never satisfy a certain proposed set of sufficient conditions for free will. And imagine there is good evidence that people sometimes do satisfy these conditions. Then that's good news for free will—provided it's plausible that the conditions really are in line with a legitimate way of thinking about what "free will" means. And the news doesn't stop being good if these conditions include something that isn't actually necessary for free will. There's nothing wrong with having good evidence for the existence of something that includes even more than what you absolutely need for free will. It's like having more money in the bank than you actually need. There's nothing wrong with that.

SALLY: I understand.

DEB: I'll start with regular free will. Suppose Zeke is a competent decision maker who hasn't been manipulated in any way relevant to a decision he is about to make and isn't compelled or coerced. He's capable of weighing reasons and making an informed decision about what to do, and he makes one on the basis of his rational assessment of pros and cons. That's enough for Zeke to have decided freely, according to this way of thinking about free will. We call fans of regular free will low-riders. People who go in for mid-grade free will are mid-graders. And those who opt for premium are top-shelfers.

SALLY: Tell me about the mid-graders and top-shelfers.

BOB: To bump up to mid-grade free will, you mix what we call deep openness into low-rider free will.

SALLY: Ah, deep openness. When Cliff called, he explained it in terms of possible worlds. If Zeke decides to go to the Sweet Shop and he has deep openness at the time, then there's another possible world where everything is the same right up until then—the entire history of the universe and all the laws of nature—and, even so, something else happens. For example, he might decide to go to your favorite coffee shop instead.

BOB: That's the idea. By the way, were you outside the coffee shop this afternoon? Cliff thought he saw you there.

SALLY: No. The closest I got was a gas station a few blocks away—one that sells diesel fuel. My car runs on diesel.

FRAN: And now to get premium free will, you mix a soul into mid-grade free will.

SALLY: And how are souls supposed to be involved in free will?

BOB: They're supposed to make free decisions, I guess.

ED: If a soul makes your decisions, then you don't. But then you don't decide freely, because you don't decide at all.

FRAN: Well, maybe you use your soul when you make free decisions. If that's how it's supposed to work, it would still be you making the decision.

CLIFF: Would you be using your soul in addition to your mind or in addition to your brain? Or would you use them together—in combination?

BOB (*SINGING*): "With the power of soul anything is possible. With the power of you anything you wanna do."

ED: I heard that song on the jukebox here earlier this week. I think the old guys played it: "Power of Soul" by Jimi Hendrix.

BOB: Maybe it's about free will. And Hendrix might be saying that you are your soul. What do you think? (*singing again*) "With the power of you anything you wanna do."

CLIFF: Questions like that make me happy I invited Sally.

BOB: Questions about Sixties music?

CLIFF: No, questions like how you're related to your soul.

BOB: And is it the questions themselves that cause you to be happy or is it subatomic events associated with your hearing them that do the causal work?

SALLY: What?

CLIFF: Never mind, Sally. That's a long story. How are you related to your soul? What's your view about that?

SALLY: Hard question, I'm afraid. There are lots of different theories about what souls are. I like the idea that your soul is whatever makes you you and it's a nonphysical thing that continues to exist after your body dies. I wouldn't say that your soul *is* you now. But it will be you after your body dies. You'll continue to exist, but in a different form—as a soul. I suppose I'd say that your soul is part of you now—the part that makes you who you are. Here's a more technical way of putting it: Right now, you're a combination of a body and a soul; but when your body dies, you'll just be your soul.

ED: I'm willing to go along with that way of understanding the word "soul," even if I don't fully understand it. I don't believe in souls, and I don't believe they're needed for free will. But I wonder why you think the existence of souls is a real possibility despite what science tells us about reality.

SALLY: And why don't you believe in souls? Just curious.

ED: I think of the idea that there are souls as a theory that's supposed to help us understand some aspect or other of what we take to be real. Imagine that Zeke believes in life after death. Then he might postulate the existence of souls in order to explain how life after death is possible. It's possible, he thinks, because a soul can exist after the body associated with it dies.

BOB: Why is it always Zeke?

DEB: Maybe because we don't know anyone named Zeke and it's an unusual name.

ED: Now, about life after death . . . If you think it happens, do you need to believe in nonphysical souls? I don't think so. If you believe in life after death, you probably also believe in God. Why can't God make special physical bodies for the afterlife? Your body dies; but just before it does, God builds everything that makes you you into a new and much improved physical body that lasts forever. And then he brings you to heaven. It seems like whatever a soul can do for you, God can do for you in this way.

DEB: Is heaven a physical place then?

ED: Why not? How would any of us know that it isn't? We've never been there, and we've never heard about it from anyone who has been there.

BOB: And what makes you you, according to you, Ed?

CLIFF: Excellent usage of "you," Bob.

ED: Well, if it isn't your actual physical body, then I think it's things housed in that body, like beliefs, memories, preferences, character traits, habits, and so on. My theory about life after death is that God builds things like this into a new body—your new body.

FRAN: Do you believe this theory, Ed?

ED: No. I don't believe in life after death. All I'm saying is that even if you do believe in life after death, you can make sense of the idea without believing in nonphysical souls.

FRAN: Got it. But we're drifting away from our topic: Do scientific findings prove that premium free will doesn't exist?

BOB: What do you think, Sally?

SALLY: Well, as I think about the souls here on Earth, they don't act, and they don't cause anything. So I don't see how their presence or absence can be detected in scientific experiments. As far as things go here on Earth, they'd go just the same way if there were no souls. What souls are needed for, as I think about things, is the afterlife.

BOB: So why do we have souls now? Why are they here?

SALLY: They need to be here in order to get there—in order to get to where God is, heaven.

CLIFF: We might have misled you a bit, Sally, when we described premium free will as mid-grade free will with a soul mixed in. What I've always been thinking is that we're mixing a soul into what fuels or powers the person, so that the soul would be involved in causing decisions.

ALICE: Me too. By the way, I've been doing some reading on theories of free will, and I ran across something else that some philosophers mix into mid-grade free will. It's called "agent causation." At first, it sounded a bit like a soul at work. But I learned that it doesn't necessarily involve souls. Even so, it brings in something you don't seem to get in mid-grade free will.

SALLY: I suppose I could tell you about soul theories according to which souls are forces or agents or have active powers. But, as I've said, I don't think of souls that way, and I'd be more interested in hearing about agent causation.

CLIFF: Go for it, Alice.

BOB: Wait a minute! How are we going to squeeze this into our gas station? We've already used regular, mid-grade, and premium.

DEB: It can be diesel fuel, Bob. Tell us about it, Alice.

ALICE: OK, here's one way to understand agent causation. Think of causation as a relation between a cause and an effect. Probably, as you normally think about causation, causes and effects are events. For example, an old air conditioner's starting up might cause lights to flicker. If that happens, the causal relation connects one event with another.

BOB: Don't jinx us, Alice. If the power shuts down the way it did last month, that event will cause many sweating events. It gets really hot in here without a/c.

ALICE: Now, in the case of agent causation, the causal relation connects the agent—the person—to an event. The event might be a decision, for example.

ED: And that isn't just a way of saying that relevant events involving the person cause the decision? Neurochemical events or conscious reasoning or whatever?

ALICE: According to agent causation theory, causation by agents is different from causation by events and it's not reducible to or definable in terms of causation by events.

BOB: How is that supposed to work? How would I cause a decision in the agent-causing kind of way?

ALICE: Sometimes it seems like they're saying that there's nothing more to say than that the agent just does cause the decision or some other action or event—that the causal relation just does connect the agent to the decision or other event.

BOB: That doesn't seem terribly illuminating. But OK. We can get back to that issue if we need to. What I'd like to know now is what's supposed to be gained by mixing agent causation into mid-grade free will.

ALICE: A solution to a problem you brought up Tuesday afternoon. You told us a story about another man named Bob to illustrate the problem. He agreed to toss a coin at noon to start a football game, but a gambler tempted him to cheat and toss it two minutes later instead. The gambler had bet that the coin toss would happen at 12:02, and he offered Bob fifty dollars to help him cheat.

CLIFF: The gambler was named Cliff, but he wasn't me. I don't gamble. Bob talked about the cheater's not being morally responsible for deciding to cheat and then linked that to the idea that he didn't freely decide to cheat.

BOB: Right. In Fran's version of my story, Bob does his best to talk himself into doing the right thing. But he decides at noon to cheat and to pretend to be searching for the coin in his pockets for two minutes. Bob has deep openness at the time, and in another possible world with the same past up to noon and the same laws of nature, his best was good enough: he decides at noon to toss the coin straightaway. This difference struck me as a lot like the difference between a coin landing heads and a coin landing tails—just a matter of luck. I went on and on about it and eventually suggested that Bob doesn't have enough control over whether he makes the bad decision or does something else instead to be morally responsible for the decision he actually makes. After all, in doing his best, Bob did the best he could do to maximize the probability (before noon) that he would decide to do the right thing, and, even so, he decided to cheat. Fran said that what Bob decides is not sufficiently up to him for Bob to be morally responsible for making the decision he makes.

FRAN: And Bob made the point that if the Bob in the story had *freely* decided to cheat, he would have been morally responsible for cheating. So I concluded that Bob's decision to cheat wasn't free and that deep openness at the time of a decision might actually rule out free decision making at that time.

ED: I wasn't entirely convinced even by Bob's much more thorough presentation of the problem on Tuesday. But that's another story. The question now is how agent causation is supposed to solve the problem.

DEB: After Bob explained what bothered him about deep openness, Alice and I asked whether premium free will might contain a solution, and Bob gave us an answer.

BOB: I said I didn't see how mixing a soul into mid-grade free will can help.

DEB: As I recall, you said that if a totally physical person doesn't have enough control over what he decides in the presence of deep openness to be morally responsible for his decision and to make his decision freely, you didn't see how adding a soul to the person helps. It's deep openness that poses the problem, not being totally physical.

BOB: Right. And as far as I can tell, the same point applies to mixing agent causation into mid-grade free will. The problem is posed by deep openness. I can't see how it matters whether the causal relation connects relevant events to a person's decision or instead connects the agent as agent-cause to his decision.

SALLY: I'm a newcomer to all this. Maybe you can say a bit more, Bob.

BOB: Well, look at it this way. Go back to those two possible worlds I talked about and add just one thing to the story: Bob agent-causes his decision. I can't see how that makes it any more up to him what he decides than it is in the original story. It seems that nothing important has changed.

SALLY: Might the agent-causation philosophers be thinking that agent causation is "up to you" causation?

BOB: If they are, I'd like to know what it is about agent causation that makes it "up to you" causation. Why is it that if the causal relation connects the agent to a decision rather than connecting events in the agent to a decision, then we have "up to you" causation?

SALLY: Did you find an answer to that question, Alice?

ALICE: Not really. Or if I did, I didn't fully understand it. Or maybe I did understand it but thought it underestimated the decision-causing power of conscious reasoning and other relevant events.

CLIFF: Well, even if we ignore the diesel and premium pumps at our gas station, we still have regular and mid-grade free will to think about. I can truly say that my own thinking about them has come a long way since Monday.

ALICE: Sally, our five-day discussion began Monday afternoon when I told Bob about an article I was reading. It said that a group of neuroscientists had proved there's no free will.

BOB: Right. I asked Alice whether she believed what the news article claimed, and that led us down the winding path that took us to where we are now.

ALICE: Our main objective was to figure out whether scientific findings rule out free will or at least provide good evidence that free will doesn't exist. Even if we don't yet understand some ways of thinking about free will well enough to go further with them, we have a better understanding of regular and mid-grade free will.

ED: And we've shown to my satisfaction at least that there's no powerful scientific evidence against the existence of free will as the low-riders or mid-graders think of it.

BOB: I agree with Ed. I have reservations about the possibility of mid-grade free will, but they aren't based on science. Also, maybe if I look into philosophical writings about this, I'll discover a solution to my problem.

FRAN: I agree with Ed too. I have the feeling low-riders set the bar for free will too low and deep openness really is required for free will. But my problems with regular free will aren't scientific ones. I suppose you'd say they're philosophical problems.

CLIFF: I think Ed's right about the interesting experiments we discussed. And, as I've said, I like compatibilism. Regular gas has always been good enough for me, and the same thing goes for regular free will.

DEB: Someday I'll take a philosophy course on free will, if I can find one. But I'm on board with the idea that, so far, science leaves the free will door wide open—at least for regular and mid-grade. I don't understand premium and diesel free will well enough to be confident how the scientific experiments apply to them.

ALICE: I'm with Deb. What about you, Sally?

SALLY: I think I want to take a course on the soul first.

BOB: Well, it's Friday night, and it looks like we're wrapping things up. Our conversations have been great, and I learned a lot about philosophy and science from all of you. I even learned something about our topics from myself, which is nice. Anyway, I'm leaving town tomorrow for a couple of weeks. I'm going to visit family and friends in New York.

ALICE: Are you in a New York state of mind?

BOB (*SINGING*): "I don't care if it's Chinatown or on Riverside. I don't have any reasons. I left them all behind."

Hendrix's "Power of Soul" starts playing on the Internet jukebox just as the air conditioner comes on. The lights flicker. Then the power goes out. Total darkness—until people start using their cigarette lighters.

BOB: I think that's a sign. Let's call it a night.

The seven friends try to find their way out of the Warehouse. The main door is stuck temporarily. People gather there until Tucker pushes it open. The friends are among the first to leave the building.

Sources

Monday Afternoon

The two sources mentioned are H. Putnam, *Reason, Truth and History* (Cambridge, UK: Cambridge University Press, 1981) and my "Premium, Mid-Grade and Regular Free Will Fuel Accountability," *Phi Kappa Phi Forum* 92 (2012): 11–12.

Monday Night

The original Frankfurt-style story appears in H. Frankfurt, "Alternate Possibilities and Moral Responsibility," *Journal of Philosophy* 66 (1969): 829–39. Deb's story about Diana and Ernie is based on a story in chapter 7 of my *Free Will and Luck* (New York: Oxford University Press, 2006).

Tuesday Afternoon

Bob's story about the cheating coin-flipper is from chapter 3 of my *Free Will and Luck* (New York: Oxford University Press, 2006). Bob's thought experiment involving a random number generator is from my "Moral Responsibility and the Continuation Problem," *Philosophical Studies* 162 (2013): 237–55. The quotation from Read Montague is from p. 584 of his "Free Will," *Current Biology* 18 (2008): R584-5. The survey study that Deb describes is from my "Free Will and Substance Dualism: The Real Scientific Threat to Free Will?" in W. Sinnott-Armstrong, ed. *Moral Psychology, Volume 4: Free Will and Responsibility* (Cambridge, Mass.: MIT Press, forthcoming).

Tuesday Night

Fran's presentation of Libet's work is based primarily on a pair of works by Libet: "Unconscious Cerebral Initiative and the Role of Conscious Will in Voluntary Action," *Behavioral and Brain Sciences* 8 (1985): 529–66, and *Mind Time* (Cambridge, Mass.: Harvard University Press, 2004). The critique of Libet's work is based mainly on chapters 2, 3, and 4 of my *Effective Intentions: The Power of Conscious Will* (New York: Oxford University Press, 2009). I'm the professor in the video who talked about silently saying "now" to himself. I discuss my brief stint as a subject in a Libet-style experiment in chapters 2 and 4 of *Effective Intentions*. Ed's ideas about conscious reasoning being in the loop even if consciousness of one's reasoned decision lags a bit behind decision making are based on my "Unconscious Decisions and Free Will," *Philosophical Psychology*, forthcoming. The go-signal reaction time study that Fran describes is from P. Haggard and E. Magno, "Localising Awareness of Action with Transcranial Magnetic Stimulation," *Experimental Brain Research* 127 (1999): 102–7.

Wednesday Afternoon

Deb's quotation from the news source is from E. Youngsteadt, "Case Closed for Free Will?" *ScienceNOW Daily News* 4/14/2008. The fMRI study described in that article is from C. Soon, M. Brass, H. Heinze, and J. Haynes, "Unconscious Determinants of Free Decisions in the Human Brain," *Nature Neuroscience* 11 (2008): 543–5. The quotations from that study are from p. 544, and the critique is based on my "Free Will and Substance Dualism: The Real Scientific Threat to Free Will?" in W. Sinnott-Armstrong, ed. *Moral Psychology, Volume 4: Free Will and Responsibility* (Cambridge, Mass.: MIT Press, forthcoming). The idea that Ann illustrates with the fable of Buridan's ass is developed in chapter 4 of my *Effective Intentions* (New York: Oxford University Press, 2009). The experiment using depth electrodes is from I. Fried, R. Mukamel, and G. Kreiman, "Internally Generated Preactivation of Single Neurons in Human Medial Frontal Cortex Predicts Volition," *Neuron* 69 (2011): 548–62, and the critique is based on my "Unconscious Decisions and Free Will," *Philosophical Psychology*, forthcoming. Fran's suggestion that the main work for conscious experience to do in various neuroscience experiments is to enable participants to make their consciousness reports is based on chapter 2 of *Effective Intentions*. The quotation from

V. S. Ramachandran is from p. 87 of his *A Brief Tour of Human Consciousness* (New York: Pi Press, 2004). Bob's critique of Ramachandran's thought experiment is based on chapter 4 of my *Effective Intentions*.

Wednesday Night

Fran's quotation from Gazzaniga is from p. 77 of his *Who's in Charge? Free Will and the Science of the Brain* (New York: HarperCollins, 2011). The critique of some of Gazzaniga's ideas is based on part of an interview I did with *3:AM Magazine:* http://www.3ammagazine.com/3am/the-4million-dollar-philosopher/. The sources for the four famous social psychology experiments discussed this evening are as follows: (the good Samaritan) J. Darley and C. Batson, "From Jerusalem to Jericho: A Study of Situational and Dispositional Variables In Helping Behavior," *Journal of Personality and Social Psychology* 27 (1973): 100–8; (bystander effect) J. Darley and B. Latané, "Bystander Intervention in Emergencies: Diffusion of Responsibility," *Journal of Personality and Social Psychology* 8 (1968): 377–83; (finding a dime) A. Isen and P. Levin, "Effect of Feeling Good on Helping: Cookies and Kindness," *Journal of Personality and Social Psychology* 21 (1972): 384–8; (nylon stockings) R. Nisbett and T. Wilson, "Telling More than We Can Know: Verbal Reports on Mental Processes," *Psychological Review* 84 (1977): 243–4.

Thursday Afternoon

Ed's written sources for Milgram's experiments are S. Milgram, "Behavioral Study of Obedience," *The Journal of Abnormal and Social Psychology* 67 (1963): 371–8, S. Milgram, "Some Conditions of Obedience and Disobedience to Authority," *Human Relations* 18 (1965): 57–76, and S. Milgram, *Obedience to Authority* (New York: Harper & Row, 1974). For the Milgram video Ed mentions, see *Introsocsite: Introduction to Sociology:* http://www.nyu.edu/classes/persell/aIntroNSF/TeacherResources/MilgramExperimentFilm.html. The journal article on the Stanford prison experiment that Ed quotes from is C. Haney, W. Banks, and P. Zimbardo, "Interpersonal Dynamics of a Simulated Prison," *International Journal of Criminology and Penology* 1 (1973): 69–97; the quotation is from p. 81. The *New York Times Magazine* article that Ed quotes from is P. Zimbardo, C. Haney, W. Banks, and D. Jaffe, "The Mind Is a Formidable Jailer: A Pirandellian Prison,"

The New York Times Magazine, Section 6 (1973, April 8: 38–60). The
online source from which he quotes is P. Zimbardo, "Stanford Prison
Experiment": http://www.prisonexp.org/.

Thursday Night

Bob's quotation from Wegner is from p. 144 of *The Illusion of Conscious
Will* (Cambridge, Mass.: MIT Press, 2002). That book is the source
for Bob's presentation of Wegner's ideas. The critique of some of
Wegner's ideas is based on chapters 2 and 5 of my *Effective Intentions*
(New York: Oxford University Press, 2009). The review articles on
implementation intentions that Bob mentions are P. Gollwitzer,
"Implementation Intentions," *American Psychologist* 54 (1999):
493–503, and P. Gollwitzer and P. Sheeran, "Implementation Intentions and Goal Achievement: A Meta-Analysis of Effects and Processes," *Advances in Experimental Social Psychology* 38 (2006): 69–119.
The discussion of the philosophical significance of implementation
intentions is based on chapter 7 of my *Effective Intentions*.

Friday Afternoon

The experiment on fruit flies that Deb mentions is from A. Maye,
C. Hseih, G. Sugihara, and B. Brembs, "Order in Spontaneous
Behavior," *PLoS ONE*, issue 5, e443 (2007): 1–14. The news article
she mentions is "Do Fruit Flies Have Free Will?" *ScienceDaily*, 2007:
http://www.sciencedaily.com/releases/2007/05/070516071806.htm.

Friday Night

No new sources were used. Readers interested in my own take on the
bearing of agent causation on free will may wish to read chapter 3 of
my *Free Will and Luck* (New York: Oxford University Press, 2006).

Glossary

Agent causation: Causation of an effect by an agent. Agent causation is neither reducible to nor definable in terms of causation by events.

Compatibilism: The thesis that free will is compatible with determinism.

Deep openness: A condition requiring the falsity of determinism in which an agent has more than one option at a time, given everything as it actually is at the time.

Determinism: The thesis that a complete description of the universe at any time together with a complete list of all the laws of nature entails everything else that's true about the universe.

Electroencephalogram (EEG): A test that measures electrical brain activity.

Entailment: A statement A entails a statement B when, necessarily, if A is true, then so is B.

Free will, diesel: Much like premium free will, except that the power of agent causation replaces soul power.

Free will, mid-grade: A mixture of regular free will and deep openness.

Free will, premium: A mixture of mid-grade free will and soul power.

Free will, regular: Associated with being an informed, competent decision maker who hasn't been manipulated in any way relevant to a decision he is about to make and isn't compelled or coerced.

Functional magnetic resonance imaging (fMRI): A technique for measuring brain activity by detecting changes in blood flow in the brain.

Implementation intention: An intention to do something at a particular place and time.

Proximal intention: An intention to do something now.

Readiness potential: A progressive increase in brain activity preceding intentional movements, normally measured using EEG.

W time: The time at which a participant in an experiment first becomes aware of an urge or intention to perform a particular action.

Index